BEAUTIFULLY BROKEN

The Story of Two Fathers Fighting to
Save Their Families and the Unlikely
Journey that Changed Them Both

RANDY HARTLEY and
WILLIAM & EBRALIE MWIZERWA

with Ken Abraham

Fedd Book
P.O. Box 341973
Austin, TX 78734

www.thefeddagency.com

Published in association with The Fedd Agency, Inc., a literary agency.

ISBN: 978-1-949784-60-2
eISBN: 978-1-949784-61-9

Library of Congress Control Number: 2020925215

Printed in the United States of America

First Edition 15 14 13 12 11 / 10 9 8 7 6 5 4 3 2

No man knows how or when the tests will come, or how far he will go to protect those he loves.

CONTENTS

Chapter 1

LIVING THE DREAM

When people view themselves as worthless, they begin to treat themselves as worthless. Their behavior often turns into a downward spiral of negativity: low self-worth inspires self-destructive behavior, causing their self-esteem to further erode, and the feedback loop continues. When the person caught in the downward spiral is your daughter—your once fun-loving, happy-go-lucky little girl— you will do anything to help. You will go anywhere to try to solve the problem. You will learn lessons from anyone who can teach them.

This is my story. This is the story of how my family—my daughters, my son, my wife, and I—was once broken. This is the story of how, through the most incredible journey, our lives became intertwined with two other families from across the globe, and our shattered pieces were put back together in a way that I could have never imagined.

We traveled the world to find ourselves. Along the way, I saw and learned of unspeakable evil—but I also saw love and kindness far more powerful than that evil. I saw how my Lord, whom I once suspected of forsaking us, had instead gone before us and had carved out a path that we could not yet see and could have never predicted. That path was filled with many "coincidences"—those minor miracles where God chose to remain anonymous at the time, but where we now look back and see God's providence in full display. Eventually, what once was shattered into shards was put back together like a mosaic of beautiful stained glass in the cathedral of life.

\\\

I grew up believing that a dad's most important job was to provide for and protect his family. That was a belief I had learned from my father. I worked hard and developed a successful career as a financial planner, and I was certain that I was doing everything I could to fulfill my responsibilities as a good husband and father. God had blessed my career and had certainly allowed me to meet my family's needs and to keep them safe. With a nice home in Brentwood, Tennessee—an upscale community just outside of Nashville—my family was tucked away in suburbia, hidden in a bubble and protected.

However, my idyllic world would be crushed one day when I learned that evil doesn't care whether you live in the suburbs or in the heart of downtown. It doesn't care if you appear to be living the American dream. Evil can find its way anywhere.

I had been raised along the bayous of south Louisiana, just north of New Orleans. My family had moved there in 1963 when my father took a job as an aeronautics engineer in the early days of the space program.

Dad thought the best place to raise a family was outside of the city. He commuted more than an hour to and from work each day for more than thirty years to give us that life that I loved, and I am very thankful and appreciative to him for it. I have nothing but fond memories of growing up in a family of five kids and a dog. My dad loved to play with us. I remember him crawling on the floor, playfully wrestling with us after work. He coached several of my sports teams, and he taught me how to hunt and fish—things he loved to do as a boy.

I loved the outdoors, too, spending countless hours in the woods and bayous. After school and especially in the summer, my mother would tell us to get out of the house, but to be sure to be back for dinner by 5:30 p.m. when my dad would be home. She didn't know where we were, and neither did the other neighborhood moms whose sons were building forts and fishing with us. But why worry? This was suburbia, and life was good. That was the life I wanted to duplicate for my own family one day.

My American dream started in 1983 when I graduated from college and moved to Tennessee. After considering opportunities in New York City and Dallas, I settled on a job with a financial-planning firm in Nashville. Fate was kind to me with that decision: I love my job so much that it is the one and only job I have ever had. Thirty-eight years later, I am still at that same firm, having worked with many of my partners for all those years.

I met my wife, Darla, just a couple of years after I moved to Nashville. Darla had grown up in the rural hills of Pendleton County,

Kentucky, where she had also been raised in a family of five children. Her dad was a farmer, but Darla excelled in school, went to the University of Kentucky, and became a pharmacist. Darla moved to Nashville five months after I did, and our paths crossed eighteen months later, in March 1985.

I was smitten right away. On our first date, we went to dinner at a restaurant and talked for hours. The poor waitress must have been frustrated with us since she wasn't able to turn the table all night.

After Darla and I had dated for a few months, she invited me to go with her to visit her family. Darla's parents still lived in the childhood home in which she had grown up, in the back hills of northern Kentucky. During that first trip, Darla guided me all around Pendleton County, showing me her elementary school and high school, the church she had attended, and the old wood-frame homes where her grandparents had lived. We began to call it the "roots" tour, and Darla seemed a bit self-conscious about her modest beginnings. Little did she know that my upbringing was not unlike hers.

A couple of months later, Darla accompanied me to visit my family, who still lived in Slidell, Louisiana, in the same home my parents had purchased when I started high school. I, too, took Darla on a "roots" tour, passing by my former schools, prior churches, and the boyhood homes where I had lived. As we made our way out to Lacombe, down Lacombe Harbor Drive, and past the moss-covered pecan grove where I lived between the ages of nine and thirteen, she looked at me and said, "You know, our roots are not that far apart." I smiled and said, "No, they just come with a slightly different accent!"

We got engaged in January 1986 and were married just five months later. It was a quick engagement by current standards, but it must have been the right decision, because Darla is still putting up with me more than thirty-five years later.

Shortly after our marriage, Darla and I moved to Brentwood, Tennessee, a suburb just south of Nashville. We knew that we would soon start a family, and Brentwood seemed like a great place to raise our children. Also, my office was in Brentwood, so living there would avoid the sacrifice of a commute that I had seen my dad make for so many years.

We bought an old craftsman bungalow in Brentwood that had been built in 1911. Although the house itself is now well more than one hundred years old, there is not a floor or wall in the home that has not been refinished or re-covered a few times. Soon after we bought the home, our family began to grow. First was the addition of our new dog, Tyson, a beautiful boxer named after the world champion boxer of that time. Then in early 1990, we had our first child—our daughter Alyssa. Two years later, our middle daughter, Andrea, was born, and four years after that, we welcomed our son, Nate. Our family was complete, and we couldn't have been happier.

Alyssa was more of our girly-girl, always making sure everything was just right and meticulously fussing to get things perfect, whether it was her clothes, her makeup, or the latest dance step that she was learning. Her bedroom was all pink and fit for a princess, and she played the part! She was a go-getter. She had a ten-year plan by age ten!

Andrea was our fun-loving Daddy's girl. She loved cheerleading and gymnastics, but she also had an independent streak. She always wanted to do things her own way. I often commented, only half-joking, "Andrea is a left-brained girl in a right-brained world." She was carefree, quick with her comments, and so funny, always coming up with the cutest sayings. Even as a little girl, she always had a heart of compassion, and she was equally as quick to stand up for the less fortunate or for a friend in trouble.

Nate, our youngest child, was highly intelligent and quieter than his sisters. He had to be—because they didn't give him much of a chance to talk! Nate grew up in the shadow of two very different sisters, so he carved his own niche in his contemplative way. He was a mix of his older sisters, excelling in school while enjoying an active social life with his buddies.

Our children spent their entire childhoods in our picturesque old craftsman home, which, as it turns out, was right in the center of the "Brentwood Bubble" that I had hoped would shelter our children and give them the same idyllic childhood I had enjoyed. Recently our children told us, "You and Mom are not allowed to move, because this is the only home we have ever known."

We attended Brentwood United Methodist Church, a large church right in the center of Brentwood and just a few minutes from our home. Darla and I had been married in Nashville, and the ceremony was led by our beloved pastor, Dr. Joe Pennel. By pure coincidence, Dr. Pennel was assigned to Brentwood United Methodist Church about the same time we moved. So although we changed churches, we got to keep our minister. When Darla and I saw him at church on occasion, I would joke with him, telling him that he tied our wedding knot really tight. He would then lean in and say, "Glad I didn't make it a slipknot!"

This church was central to our family's life. It is where Alyssa was baptized as a baby. Andrea missed out on the typical infant baptism, however, so when it was Nate's turn to be christened, four-year-old Andrea joined with him. Darla bought her a beautiful white gown with a small headband of white flowers. During the final hymn at the end of the service, Dr. Pennel invited our family to the front of the sanctuary so the congregation could wish us well after the service. As that closing hymn played, Andrea began to dance and twirl, mesmerized by the way her gown would fill with air when she spun in circles. My first impulse was to pull her to my side and make her be still, but I did not want to make a scene.

Then I noticed that the entire congregation was watching Andrea in her own four-year-old world, twirling and dancing to the music. Everyone was smiling, enjoying the simple innocence of this precious child dancing in her baptism gown like a little angel for all to see. There is an adage that says, "Dance like no one is watching," and Andrea had clearly taken that to heart.

I have thought back to that moment many times over the years. It represented so much of what every dad wants for his children. It was fun, carefree innocence, made even more special when I consider that she was dancing in the eyes of the Lord. It was impossible to know then that, several years later, our world would careen so far away from those idyllic moments.

Chapter 2

THE ROLE OF COMPASSION

L ife is like a real-life Rube Goldberg machine, where the whole
picture, with each of its interconnected steps, is only visible to
God. Only in hindsight can we humans see how one initial step led
to an outcome we never expected. Well, my family, the Hartley family, was about to take that first step that would eventually lead us
into an unimaginable maze, only to find that the destination was far
better than we could have ever guessed. At times we were confused,
felt that we were lost in life's maze, and found it difficult to "keep the
faith." But looking back now, we realize that God was truly the Great
Creator of our life's puzzle, and He had given us the tools to solve it.

In December 1998, Darla and I went to an Amy Grant Christmas
concert. We enjoyed many of Amy's hits, along with wonderful

Christmas favorites. In the middle of her set, Amy surprised us by stopping and asking the crowd to look under their seats. There, she said, we would find information about Compassion International, a Christian organization that provided financial and spiritual support for children around the world. Inspired by the season of giving, Darla and I decided we wanted to be a part of this ministry.

We took the brochure home, gathered the kids, and told them about our idea to "adopt" and support a child from somewhere in the world. Our idea was for each of our kids to sponsor a child who was their same age and gender so that Alyssa, Andrea, and Nate could better relate to the children we would sponsor.

Alyssa, the oldest, said she wanted to support a girl from Asia. Andrea chose to support a girl from Africa. Nate decided to support a boy from South America. We completed the brochure, sent in our information, and eagerly waited to see who we would be assigned.

Within a couple of weeks, we received our new sponsor packets from Compassion International. Alyssa was connected with Subbu, an eight-year-old girl from India. Andrea was assigned to Umuhoza, a six-year-old girl from Rwanda. Nate was assigned to Henry, a young boy his age from Ecuador. We encouraged Alyssa and Andrea to write to their children, and we helped Nate compose a letter for Henry.

The Compassion International relationships soon became an exciting part of our family routine. We included these three precious children in our nightly prayers with our own children, and the letters were especially special to us. They were processed through Compassion, so we could see the actual letters as written by the children, along with the English translation of those letters.

Alyssa maintained a consistent pen-pal relationship with Subbu, although she was the first of our sponsored children to graduate out of the program. In the Compassion program, all monitored communication between the sponsors and the child normally stops once a child finishes secondary school. I will never forget Subbu's "exit" letter. Subbu thanked Alyssa for all of her support, noting all of the educational, financial, and spiritual support that she had received through the years. But it was her closing statement that really tugged at my heart. Subbu ended her last letter by saying, "Someday you may forget who I am. But I can assure you, even years from now, I will never forget you or what you have done for me."

Nate communicated with a carousel of various boys through the years, as his pen pals unfortunately kept dropping out of the program. As a result, it was difficult for him to develop a meaningful relationship with any of the children whom he supported.

Umuhoza, Andrea's girl, was from Murambi, Rwanda. We started supporting her in 1998, when both girls were six years old. Our information said that Umuhoza's father was in prison and that Umuhoza was the oldest child in her family. We knew that Rwanda had endured the terrible genocide of 1994 only a few years earlier. Virtually all Compassion projects in Rwanda had been closed during that time, and many of their children and staff had lost their lives. At the time that Andrea first connected with Umuhoza, Compassion was just beginning to be reestablished in the country.

In the beginning, most of the letters Andrea received from Umuhoza were what I called "formula" letters. She would mostly include statements such as "It's the dry season here" or "I've been helping my mother with chores." Eventually, though, as more communication went back and forth, the letters became more personal.

One intriguing detail included in each of Umuhoza's letters was an update on her goats. Our gifts through Compassion allowed her family to purchase these goats, and she was always quick to give us the latest news on the goats' well-being. This seemed funny to us at the time because we did not fully comprehend the importance of the goats in Umuhoza's impoverished existence. All we knew was that her goats were either pregnant, in good health, or doing poorly, so we sometimes whimsically referred to her letters as our "goat updates."

Andrea informed Umuhoza that she had a pet hamster named Peanut. Knowing that the purpose of goats or any animals in Rwanda was primarily utilitarian, I imagined that Umuhoza was quite perplexed as to why Andrea would own a hamster. After all, how much milk or meat could you get from a hamster?

Andrea continued her pen-pal relationship with Umuhoza as both girls approached their teenage years. One day, as Andrea was reading one of Umuhoza's letters, she turned to me and asked, "Hey, Daddy, can we go and visit Umuhoza someday?"

I was struck by the enthusiasm and sincerity of Andrea's request. Without giving it much thought, I said, "Sure, Baby. We'll go someday." It was a rather flippant reply. After all, I didn't think we would ever have the time or occasion to make a trip to Rwanda. Little did I know that the Master had a far greater plan for my family and me.

Chapter 3

TROUBLE IN PARADISE

Parents can usually tell when something is off with one of their children, but they can't always put their finger on the source of the problem—and that can make it difficult to know if the issue is a typical teenage spat or something far more serious.

Andrea had always been our more carefree child. She did well in school, but getting great grades failed to motivate her. She enjoyed her friends, was always very social, and was quite creative. We called her our flower child.

One day when Andrea was in the third grade, as her class lined up for recess, one of her friends got out of line and moved over to talk with Andrea. The principal walked by and admonished the friend, "Do you think you are special? Get back in line, please." Andrea instantly replied, "But sir, we are all special in our own way!" The principal decided that Andrea's statement was too "sassy," and he ordered her to his office, but when Darla and I learned about the incident, we knew it was just Andrea being her carefree self, standing up for a friend.

Once Andrea became a teenager, however, her innocent, carefree nature began to change. Darla and I sensed that something was wrong, but we could not identify any reason for Andrea's aberrant attitudes and actions. At first, we thought this must be normal behavior for a daughter moving into and through her adolescent years.

Alyssa, our oldest daughter, had also become a bit moody as a teen, but she hadn't acted out the way that Andrea did. Alyssa had always been more focused on achieving her goals. Active in both gymnastics and dance, she told us once as a freshman in high school, "I want to graduate from high school, attend the University of Tennessee, make the dance team, major in kinesiology, and become a physical therapist." She moved purposefully along that path, accomplishing her plan with each step, earning a full scholarship to UT and becoming a physical therapist, just as she had planned.

Andrea admired her sister immensely, but she said on occasion, "There must be something wrong with me. Alyssa knows exactly what she wants to do, and I have no idea what I want."

I would try to console her, telling her, "Andrea, you are not the one who is unusual. Alyssa is. Most people your age have no idea what they want to do. As a boy in Louisiana, I had no idea I'd be a financial planner in Nashville. Don't worry about it. You'll find what matters to you."

But Andrea continued to change. Between the time of her thirteenth and sixteenth birthdays, her surly behavior grew increasingly more intense. At first, it was just an attitude—the way she would talk, or act, or the tone in which she would answer our questions or requests—but more and more, she turned inward, moving away from Darla, her siblings, and me while gravitating to a group of new friends with whom we were unfamiliar.

I wanted to think that it was just a phase she was going through, but Darla felt there was something more. Part of what blurred my vision was my own ability to compartmentalize various sections of my life. An optimistic person by nature, I had trained myself from my early years to focus on the positive aspects of my experience and shut out the negative. For instance, when my parents divorced during my senior year of high school, I refused to allow my sadness to pull me down. As much as I hated my parents' divorce, I said, "It's my senior year, and I'm not going to let Mom and Dad's breakup ruin my life. That's *them*, and I know it will affect me, but not all the time. I am going to put that into a drawer. I will open the drawer and worry about it for a time, but then I will put it back in the drawer again and not think about it."

I've always viewed life as a series of drawers: it is up to me to open or close them. While I am at work, I open the "business" drawers and close all the others. Then after work, by the time I get in the car and travel the short distance from the office to our home, I have shut all the business drawers and opened the "husband" and "dad" and "family" drawers.

That system always worked well for me, but my ability to compartmentalize also led to blind spots in truly seeing what was happening as Andrea was going through her turbulent teenage years. I didn't understand her emotions, and I wanted so much to have a positive attitude that I could not allow myself to see what was going on with Andrea.

Darla is different. She is intuitive, and unlike me, who was working fifty hours a week outside the home, she was around Andrea more often. The more time they spent together, the more certain Darla became that we were headed for trouble. She knew something was wrong with Andrea, and she was right. But we never could have imagined what it was.

Chapter 4

THE
DARK SIDE

Andrea started to assert even more independence during her junior year in high school. With Alyssa now in college, Andrea turned more easily to partying. She was now driving herself to school and was better able to do what she pleased without having her big sister looking over her. That gave Andrea plenty of opportunity to make poor decisions.

At home, her room became a dark hole. Darla had to constantly remind her to clean it up since she usually left her bed unmade and cast her clothes in every direction. She kept the drapes closed most of the time, casting a pall across her brightly decorated space and turning everything in it a muted gray.

The constant stress Darla and I felt over Andrea created palpable tension in our own relationship with each other. We knew we loved each other and were committed to each other, but questions nagged at us. What were we doing wrong? Why couldn't we get through to our daughter? At times, Darla complained that I was too lenient with Andrea, and I countered that she was too strict. At other times, we would switch opinions, both of us clawing for anything we could hang on to that might explain what was happening—and even more importantly, make it better. Meanwhile, Andrea's eyes looked as though the light in them had gone out. Our little girl, whom we loved so much, was turning into somebody neither of us knew.

Conflict between Andrea and Darla, Andrea and me, or Darla and me got to be an almost daily ordeal, exacerbated by Andrea's increasingly belligerent disobedience. On one occasion, Andrea told us that she was at a friend's house, but when I drove by the house to check on her, she was nowhere in sight. I repeatedly knocked on the door, but no one answered. As I turned to leave, I could see the friend watching me from her upstairs bedroom window. Suddenly my phone rang; Andrea called to admit that she had lied to me. When she confessed that she was actually at the movies with a boy, I demanded that she get home immediately.

As I stood waiting in our driveway, I saw a pickup truck coming up the road. It stopped about two houses away. Andrea hopped out and ran through the yard to our house, oblivious to my presence in the driveway.

"Andrea!" I yelled, as she started to run past me.

She jumped in surprise.

"Who was that guy?" I demanded.

"He's just some guy you don't know."

"Why didn't he drop you off at our house?" I yelled.

"Because I was afraid you would make a scene," she replied.

"Well, any guy who thinks he is man enough to take you out," I said, making a scene, "should be man enough to come face the music when he is caught. No boy worth anything should throw you out of his truck like a newspaper!"

I was furious. Andrea had lied to us. She had tried to sneak past us, and she didn't seem to see why this was wrong. I grounded her, of course, but it seemed to make no difference in her disposition. Unfortunately, the problems only escalated.

Another time, Andrea was supposed to be spending the night at the house of her friend Alicia. Again, something about the situation did not feel right, so I called Alicia's house to make sure Andrea was there. No one answered, but my phone rang a few minutes later.

"You called?" Andrea said innocently.

"Yes, I just wanted to make sure that you were at Alicia's house."

"Yep, we're here," Andrea replied.

As I asked more questions, something in me told me she was lying, so I asked Andrea to tell me the truth. "You are telling me that if I get in the car and drive to Alicia's house, you will be able to come out on the porch to let me see that you are there."

"Yes." She insisted that she was there.

"Okay," I said. "I'm driving over. Be ready to come out on the porch where I can see you."

I felt bad for not trusting my daughter, but I hopped in the car and quickly made the four-minute drive to Alicia's house. When I got there, the house was dark. I called Alicia's phone number, but nobody answered.

Soon my phone rang. It was Andrea. "Dad, I'm not at Alicia's."

I was furious. *How could Andrea be so bold as to lie to me, knowing I was driving over to check on her?*

Andrea admitted that she was at a party. She had gone with some friends but didn't know where the house was located. I demanded that she find someone who could tell me where they were, and I told her I was coming to get her.

It turned out that the friends Andrea was with were from a different school, and they were not people she usually hung out with. Eventually, someone got on the phone but could only give directions that were oriented from his high school, so I had to first drive ten miles to that school. He then began to give me directions, and I soon realized that I was driving back to where I started. The party was in a neighborhood right next to Alicia's house, but the guy had me take a twenty-mile round trip to get there.

I was incensed when I finally got to the party location. I told Andrea on the phone, "You better meet me at the road, as you surely do not want me coming into the house!"

Sure enough, as I pulled up, Andrea came running from the house and met me curbside. "I'm sorry! I'm so sorry!"

I could barely contain my anger. I could not believe that she would disrespect me so much as to repeatedly lie right to my face, and then send me on a wild goose chase at midnight trying to find her. We drove home in dead silence.

I grounded Andrea again. Darla and I were at our wits' end trying to figure out a way to get through to her. We imposed a strict curfew, and we no longer allowed her to spend nights out for sleepovers with friends. We took away her access to the car, and we took away her phone as well.

Andrea's actions and attitudes improved a bit over the next few weeks, and Darla and I dared to believe we had turned a corner. It turned out that we had, but not in the direction we were hoping.

Chapter 5

NEARING ROCK BOTTOM

Andrea was grounded for much of the first semester of her junior year for various violations of our home rules, including breaking curfew and getting poor grades, along with other attitude and obedience issues. Her behavior seemed better, though, as we approached Christmas break.

Our oldest daughter, Alyssa, came home from college for a few days around Christmastime, but her dance team was scheduled to perform at a University of Tennessee basketball game back in Knoxville during the holidays. We wanted to spend as much time as we could with her, given the short time we had, so we planned to drive with her as a family to attend the UT game and then bring her back home for a few more days.

Andrea was still grounded, so we assumed that she would accompany us on the six-hour round trip to Knoxville. At the last minute, though, Andrea said that she didn't feel well and didn't want to go. She begged us not to make her go. I had a bad feeling about her insistence to stay home, but it didn't seem worth fighting about.

"Okay," I relented. "We're going to the game, but remember that you are grounded. I'm going to call you every so often to make sure you are at home, so you better answer every call."

"Oh yeah. I will, Dad," Andrea said nonchalantly. "I'm not going anywhere."

We went on to Knoxville, and true to my word, I called Andrea every hour or so, and she answered my calls promptly. After we had arrived at the game, I continued to call, and Andrea answered each call. Then, as we were about to head home, she didn't answer. I called again, but she still did not answer. I redialed, and still no answer. A gut-wrenching feeling swept over me as I continued to call her. Still no answer.

That night, when we were about an hour away from Nashville, Alyssa received a call from one of her friends, telling her that Andrea was at a party. Worse yet, she was drunk and out of control. "You need to come and get your sister."

My first reaction was sheer fury. *How could she do this?* I raged within. *So blatantly disobeying me, after all I had done for her, and after I had trusted her!*

I stomped down on the gas pedal and sped toward home as fast as I dared to drive. In the meantime, Alyssa made some calls and found a friend who convinced Andrea to let her give her a ride home.

We made it before Andrea. When she finally came in, she was so drunk she could barely make it up the stairs to her bedroom. Darla and I followed her. Darla was trying to steady her, and I vented.

Andrea, giddily drunk, flopped down onto her bed, and I really let her have a piece of my mind. "How could you do this to us? You are in so much trouble, young lady! What in the world do you think you are doing?"

She rolled over on her side, leaned up, and glared at me in her drunken stupor. Then, with almost a grin on her face, she said, "You are so blind." She slumped back down on the bed and shut her eyes.

I was stunned for a moment. Andrea's words seared my heart. I knew we had a deeper problem than her drinking, but I couldn't imagine what it was. I was furious at my daughter, but her statement and actions scared me. What did she mean? It was all so frustrating and heartbreaking!

One Saturday night in the spring, after a couple months of relative peace, Darla and I went out to dinner with friends. Andrea's curfew was 10:00 p.m., so she was supposed to be home when we got back. With Alyssa away at college and Nate spending the night at a friend's house, we told Andrea that we would see her when we got back.

After a nice dinner, Darla and I returned home and went to check on Andrea. We suddenly had a sinking feeling as we realized that Andrea was not there. Every time we thought that our family might be back on track, it happened again! We immediately started calling her, leaving messages, warning her that she had better get back to us immediately. Before long, the calls of anger turned into pleas of desperation. We called her friends and their parents, asking if anyone could tell us Andrea's whereabouts. No one knew where she was, and our desperation melded into pure fear.

All our calls proved futile, but I just couldn't sit around the house and wait. "I'm going to look for her," I told Darla.

"Where are you going to look?" she asked.

"I have no idea," I admitted. "But I've got to do something."

Nothing is worse for a parent than knowing your daughter is out there—somewhere—but you don't know where she is or even if she is okay. I didn't know if we would find her dead somewhere, or if we would find her at all. I would get a text from time to time, and each time I hoped it was from Andrea. Instead, the messages were from people replying to me saying they hadn't seen her. I would stop and text Andrea again, hoping that she would respond this time.

I drove around and looked for Andrea. I don't know for sure how long I drove around, but after a while, I found myself back at our house. I blinked back the tears as I prayed, *Lord, I've tried, but I just can't fix this. I am putting Andrea in Your hands. Please bring her home to us.*

Out of options and running out of hope, we called the Brentwood Police Department. I told the officer the situation. He said there wasn't much they could do at that point, but he said he would keep an eye out and do what he could. He told us that he had heard about a big party on the edge of town, and he would see if he could find out if she was there.

Darla and I went to bed at our home that night—and Andrea didn't. We waited up, still calling and texting, looking for any response from Andrea or one of her friends—or, God forbid, from a hospital or police station. It was long after midnight when we finally went to bed. However, sleep was far from me. I lay in the bed, staring at the ceiling. I prayed, wondering where she could be. There was no worse moment in the world than lying there wondering about my little girl. Finally, after several hours of tossing and turning, I drifted off to a fitful sleep sometime before dawn.

As soon as we awakened the next morning, we checked Andrea's room. She was nowhere to be found. There were no responses to the messages I had left on her phone.

We spent the morning doing more of the same—reaching out to anyone who might have an idea where Andrea could be—searching, texting, calling, and praying.

I realized that we could no longer pretend that Andrea's issues were those of a typical teen. No parent wants to admit that they can't control their teen daughter. No parent wants to think that they can't handle a situation. However, our family was nearing rock bottom, and I realized we desperately needed help. I had always viewed myself as a problem solver, but this was a battle we had fought for more than a year, and the problem was worse than ever.

I knew this time that if Andrea made it home, we could not do the same old thing and hope it would work. Grounding her, taking her car away, yelling at her—none of that was changing anything, and our family was exhausted. This time, we would need much more help.

Even though I didn't know where Andrea was, I looked up the phone number for Cumberland Heights, a thirty-day residential rehabilitation and treatment center near Nashville that provided counseling about drugs and alcohol. Cumberland Heights had a great reputation, and I prayed that they would have some answers to our desperate problems.

The male voice on the line at Cumberland Heights was calming and reassuring. He counseled me that when we found Andrea, we should not yell and fight with her. Instead, he said, we should let her know that we realize something is wrong and that we, as a family, need help in solving the problem. The counselor advised, "Don't wait to bring her. If she comes home and is willing to come, bring her immediately." I thanked him for his advice and told him that I hoped I would see him that day.

Morning turned to afternoon, and we still hadn't heard from Andrea. My frantic thoughts were racing. *Is she hurt and lying in a ditch somewhere? Should we call the police again?*

It was such a helpless feeling, and my emotions weren't helping. I bounced back and forth between despair and anger at Andrea's foolish actions, wondering what we could have ever done to have caused our beautiful daughter to rebel against her loving parents and family and to behave like this.

I texted her one more time: "Andrea, Mom and I love you, and we know you need help. Please come home and let Mom and me help you."

Within thirty seconds of that last text, my phone rang. It was Andrea. She sounded exhausted as she said, "I'm coming home, and you are right: I do need help."

There was no value in excoriating Andrea for her actions. We had done that before, to no avail. Instead, we simply welcomed the unrepentant prodigal home. "We love you, Andrea," Darla and I said to her again and again, "and we are going to find help."

Chapter 6

THE LETTER THAT CHANGED EVERYTHING

That afternoon, we drove Andrea out to Cumberland Heights. We still did not understand the cause of Andrea's recalcitrance, so we hoped that the Cumberland Heights counselors could help figure out the root of the problem that had avoided all of our attempts at discovery.

The thirty-minute drive was mostly quiet, interrupted by soft words of encouragement to Andrea. She seemed nervous but accepting that this was right for her. When we arrived, we were ushered to the admitting area, and soon the tedious check-in process momentarily distracted us from the strong emotions that we all shared.

When it was time for Andrea to go, Darla and I each gave her a long, heartfelt hug and praised her for taking this important step. It wasn't until Andrea disappeared behind a doorway to the residential hall that Darla and I burst into tears. It was painful to admit that our little girl needed rehabilitation, but there was also an awkward relief that for the first time in quite a while, we didn't have to worry about what Andrea was doing.

Andrea immediately began her needed therapy and quickly acclimated to her new surroundings. Darla and I attended weekly sessions there, too, learning about addiction and how to respond to a child who might be influenced by an addiction. During one of the sessions, the counselors told us to tell Andrea everything that she had done that had hurt us and the family. "Don't hold back," they said. "She needs to understand the hurt and harm she has caused." They added, "Don't do anything to comfort her. That will come later, but the purpose of today's exercise is to open her eyes to the pain she has caused."

That day was so difficult. Darla and I took no joy in the exercise. We were led into a large meeting room and joined other parents who had children in the same program as Andrea. The parents sat on one side of the room and the children sat on the other, with a set of chairs facing each other in the middle of the floor. One by one, each set of parents faced their child and read to them their most painful memories of the last few years. It was so hard to hear the stories of each family—stories that were all too familiar. Soon it was our turn to face Andrea.

It was gut-wrenching as a dad to be sitting across from my little girl, telling her so many things that surely hurt her so much. She was still my Andrea—the same girl who had twirled in her white baptism dress for all of the church to see—my beautiful Andrea who had so much potential. Sure, the last couple of years had been horrendously hard, but a father's love is unconditional, and my thoughts were about the little girl I had known all her life, not the tormented child of the last few years.

By the time the session was over, we were all sobbing. I wanted so badly to hug Andrea, to tell her how much I loved her, and to tell her it would all be better—but we were instructed not to do any of that. Instead, when we were finished exposing all of the hurt and pain, we were told to simply walk out of the room. Honestly, I didn't know if Andrea would respond positively. We had been cautioned to keep our expectations in check, having been told that many initial rehabilitation stays were not successful. The possibility of Andrea relapsing scared me to death.

All I could do was trust the counselors and pray that this exercise and this whole experience could somehow uncover the fun-loving, free-spirited girl who somehow had become buried under such darkness. Darla and I prayed very intensely during this time. We had always been people of prayer, but now we sought the Lord without ceasing, calling out to Him intensely and desperately: *Lord, I want my daughter back. Please show me the way. Show me what I need to do!* My Lord knew what to do, and He had already laid the trail; I just didn't know it yet.

We continued going to Cumberland Heights for regular meetings with Andrea and her counselors. During the third week of treatment, the receptionist led Darla and me to the small, white-walled, nondescript office where Andrea was waiting with her therapist. We had previously met in family rooms in the front of the facility but thought nothing of the change of venue. We felt that Andrea was doing better, but we didn't know for sure. We were anxious to see her and hear what the counselor had to say. After a few brief formalities, the counselor said to Darla and me, "Andrea has something she wants to share with you."

That's all the warning we received before hearing the news that would help make the past four years make sense and would shape the future still to come.

Andrea looked tense and quite emotional, with tears already trickling from her eyes as she handed us a handwritten letter on notebook paper. Because of her emotions, I assumed it was some sort of confession that said something like, "I'm sorry, Mom and Dad, but this is what I have done." The letter was nothing like that.

Andrea sat motionless as Darla and I held the letter and read it together. "I know you have been wondering what has been going on," the letter began. "When I was twelve years old, I was molested at Crockett Park at the city Fourth of July celebration."

As I was reading, Andrea's words bypassed my mind and seared directly into my heart. Andrea's account flashed us back to our hometown Fourth of July celebration nearly four years earlier. Probably because Andrea and her girlfriends were almost teens and didn't want to be "smothered" by their parents, they had asked to go to the park to watch the fireworks by themselves. They were getting older, and the Brentwood Bubble was a really safe place to live.

So just before dusk, I drove Andrea and several of her friends to the park. As I had predicted, thousands of people, replete with blankets and picnic baskets, dotted the grass-covered hillsides that rose up from the stage area and formed a natural amphitheater. From where

I dropped them off, I could see red, white, and blue bunting and bal-loons, and balloons, and families enjoying hotdogs, hamburgers, and ice cream. A band was playing oldies hits, while little kids ran and laughed, played on the swing sets that were tucked behind the trees, and rolled as far as they could down the hillside. It seemed happy. It seemed safe.

"Have a good time," I said to Andrea and her girlfriends as they exited the car, "and be careful; don't get too close to the fireworks."

The Fourth of July celebration was an annual tradition, beloved by Brentwood families, and this crowded park was familiar and fre-quently used. It was not some isolated, seedy part of town. It was not a place where bad things happened.

But this time, they did.

As I looked up from the letter to look into Darla's eyes, a mish-mash of questions and emotions collided and crashed in my mind. I tried desperately to maintain my composure. My heart pounded in my chest, but I felt as if I could break open at any moment.

Andrea's letter went on to say that she was sorry for not telling us and that she didn't want to hurt us. Before we finished reading, Andrea was already sobbing. We got up off the couch, moved to Andrea, and wrapped her in our arms—all of us weeping.

I don't remember anything else that anyone said after that, but I know that reading Andrea's letter crushed us. How could this have happened to our little girl? Then the realization hit me that my poor daughter had been carrying this dark secret, all on her own, for years. We soon learned that Andrea did not want to tell us what happened when the events first occurred because she thought she would be in trouble. Then she didn't want to tell us because she didn't want to hurt us. Hurt *us*! I couldn't imagine the hurt that my child had borne all this time as she tried to keep it locked inside of her rather than letting us endure the hurt of knowing our little girl had been molested.

As emotionally devastating as it was, at least this revelation gave us someplace to start. Now, for the first time in years, we could better understand the root cause of what Andrea had been going through and the silent pain she carried inside. In a strange way, it gave us reason for hope. Now we had something we could deal with—something solid to rebuild on. We could pray and seek guidance with a sense of clarity, and we could begin to move forward.

Andrea, too, seemed to feel some relief simply from revealing to us what had happened. I think she realized that she had believed a lie—thinking that we would be angry or disappointed with her. Thankfully, her counselor pressed her to open up. The counselor advised Andrea, "You have to tell your parents. It's the only way they are going to understand. And you can't keep holding on to your secret. Otherwise, you are going to keep making the same mistake."

As Andrea recounted the story to us in the counselor's office, she provided sparse details. It would be nearly six more years before Andrea disclosed further information regarding the indignities she had suffered. Eventually, Andrea revealed a poignant key to understanding her subsequent actions—actions and attitudes that nearly destroyed her life and severely impacted our entire family. Speaking of the molestation with deep emotion, Andrea said, "I did nothing about it. I let it happen. And the guilt I had for letting it happen sat with me for a long time—for years. I remember thinking that night, *Well, Andrea, you've decided that you are a bad kid, so that's the kind of girl you will be.* I sought out that destiny from then on; I got involved in drinking, partying, and drugs."

"That's it," she had decided when she came home from the park that night. "The die has been cast. I guess I'm a bad girl."

To me, that was one of the most devastating effects of the attack on our daughter. To think that the perverted acts of some other person could crush her spirit, rob her of her dignity and self-respect, and have such powerful repercussions in her life angered me and decimated me at the same time.

After we read her letter, we assured Andrea repeatedly that we loved her. After Andrea left the room, Darla and I stayed and talked with the counselor for an hour or so, but I spent most of the time trying to force my brain to process the information we had learned.

The counselor cautioned Darla and me—especially me: "Don't ask for details. If she wants to reveal more details to you, she will. But if you ask for details, it will give the impression to her that you are more concerned about the details of what happened than you are about the pain she experienced. You probably have a million questions, and that is natural, but it is not important. What matters is that it happened, and we have to get past it."

That was hard for me to swallow. I wanted to know who had hurt my daughter. How, when, and where had this happened? I wanted to go after the person who had done this to her and make them pay.

"You can actually do more damage by asking those kinds of questions," the counselor cautioned. "Even if you say, 'What happened?' it is almost as if you are attempting to assess blame or fault, probing to see if she did something wrong."

As I sat there processing all that I had learned, one of the reasons for Andrea's yearslong silence was especially hard to handle: "I didn't want to disappoint them," she had explained to the counselor. *She didn't want to disappoint us?* That devastated me. To think that our little girl would carry that heavy burden of guilt, shame, and pain for so long because she didn't want to let down her parents shook me to my core. What kind of a dad was I that my daughter couldn't come to me when she was hurting so badly? Andrea had said that she felt as if she were fighting a battle alone while wearing the happy face people expected of you in the Brentwood Bubble.

I had always thought that our family was accepting and nonjudgmental of each other. We talked easily about anything, so the questions nagged at me: *Why would Andrea not come to us immediately for help or comfort or solace? Why did she want to hide out within herself? What had we done wrong?*

Darla, too, beat herself up as a parent over what had happened to Andrea. Part of what made her pain worse was the fact that Darla herself had been a victim of sexual assault when she was about fifteen years old. "I thought at the time," she said, "that if I told my parents, my dad would have killed me. I was in a car with a guy who was not good for me. And I was drinking—not much, but anything would have been too much for my dad. When my friends left, the guy I was with told me, 'I know where they went.' It was a trick, as he led me back to a wooded area where he attacked me. I could see the devil in his eyes."

For years she wondered, *Did he do this to other people? Could I have saved other victims from his inappropriate advances?* But she was afraid to tell anyone. "I knew my parents would have responded poorly," Darla said, "so Andrea's experiences caused me to relive my own assault."

Darla told me later that the questions that plagued her were similar to my own: *How did this happen to my daughter? How did I not see the signs after it did happen? How could I not have protected her better? I've been through it, so how can I help my daughter to get through this?*

Despite the heartbreak we felt in coming to grips with Andrea's pain, knowing the truth finally shed some light on what had been going on for more than three years. I'm thankful that Darla and I could hold on to one another, because the tensions in our home placed an enormous stress on our marriage. But Darla was strong, a quiet rock of strength in my life, and God answered our prayers.

One thing I learned about Andrea's struggles caused by her molestation was how keeping it a secret caused so much additional emotional damage. I have truly come to understand that evil thrives in darkness and that shame is the bridesmaid of evil. When we keep things such as sexual abuse and molestation in the dark, we begin to believe the lies of evil. We believe it is our fault. We believe that we deserve what happened. We believe that our destiny has been determined by someone else's actions. It is only by shining light on the issue that those lies are exposed. As painful as the short term can be when exposing the issue, illuminating the darkness in our past ultimately gives us freedom over the shame.

As a society, we would prefer to talk about our accomplishments and successes. We would so much rather discuss good grades, sports successes, or the fun of a fabulous vacation. Social media can reinforce the idea that everyone else is doing great, so I better hide my scars.

However, our stories can be told in the context of overcoming pain, and then suddenly the story of pain can become one of hope. We can show our scars as battle wounds of victory. One of the first things Jesus did after He died on the cross and was resurrected was to show His disciples His scars. He did not remind them of the pain He had endured on the cross, but He reminded them of the victory over it!

God never wastes our pain. He will always bring good from it—but we have to let Him.

Chapter 7

TWO STEPS FORWARD, THREE STEPS BACKWARD

After going through Cumberland Heights's intense thirty-day residential treatment program, Andrea returned home and went back to high school to finish her junior year. Darla and I were hopeful: there was a spark back in her life, and she seemed to be doing really well. We were grateful, too, that Andrea seemed to embrace the after-care program sponsored by Cumberland Heights, receiving further guidance and checking in periodically with her counselor.

Of course, we had been warned that her recovery, like virtually all recoveries, would not simply be a smooth ride. Indeed, it was not without its setbacks.

For the junior prom in April, one of Andrea's good friends planned to have an after-party at her house, so we called the young lady's parents in advance to clarify details. The parents were aware of Andrea's recent treatment and seemed supportive of our concerns. "Oh, yes. We're going to be here," they said. "Not a problem." They assured us that they would be home all night and would chaperone the party.

The next morning, we received a call from a friend we had met at Cumberland Heights: "I just want to let you know that there are pictures out there on Facebook with the kids drinking at a prom party last night." We looked at the photos, and sure enough, Andrea and other sixteen-to-eighteen-year-olds were there drinking together.

When I confronted Andrea about it, she said, "Dad, it was not a problem. The parents knew we were drinking. They locked us in the basement and took all the car keys so we couldn't go out on the roads or get hurt in any way."

I couldn't believe what I was hearing. "Besides the fact that it is illegal to have alcohol at your age," I said, "what makes you think you are ready to handle alcohol consumption when you are less than sixty days out of Cumberland Heights?"

Like many people who go through rehabilitation programs, Andrea naïvely assumed that the battle was over, that she was able to handle whatever life throws at her now.

Those parents, whom we trusted, had allowed our daughter, who had only recently returned from a rehabilitation center, drink under their watch. In addition to that, Andrea didn't seem to think it was a big deal. It was one thing for a sixteen-year-old to make a poor decision, but I could not believe that the parents of Andrea's friend would allow this to happen. It was bad enough that they thought the responsible thing to do was to let the kids stay in their basement to drink, but even worse, they knew Andrea had just come out of treatment. They knew we expected them to supervise the kids. What kind of parent would tell us things would be fine and then let that happen? Unfortunately, we later discovered that these parents were not unusual. It is hard enough trying to keep up with high school kids, but now we had to keep an eye on the parents too!

The prom incident made clear to us the painful reality that even though the root of the issue had been revealed, that alone did not solve all of Andrea's problems. Granted, things were much better compared to life before rehab, but our days were not without their setbacks. Andrea's acting out looked different now, but she was still a teenager learning to process and respond to difficult life experiences. She would put forth a poor effort in school, miss an aftercare meeting, or talk back to her mother. These were not major things but were just enough to keep everyone in our home tiptoeing on eggshells, always afraid that the next setback would set Andrea on the downward spiral. We had been warned repeatedly that a major relapse was almost inevitable, and that thought frightened us.

One day in late spring of 2009, I came home from work to find Darla worked up about Andrea's latest misstep. It was not unusual to come home to tension as we all tried to process and adjust to everything we had been through, but on this particular day, I remember being immediately exhausted by the circumstances. *When will things ever return to normal?* I wondered.

In the midst of that frustration, I went over to the counter where Darla laid the daily mail. As I sifted through the normal bills and catalogues, something caught my eye. It was the familiar cream-colored envelope that we had been receiving for more than ten years—a letter from Compassion International. As I opened it, I discovered a letter from Umuhoza. In spite of all that Andrea had been through, she still maintained an occasional correspondence with her pen pal.

Something about that letter hit me like a bolt of lightning. I don't know why exactly, but I was suddenly struck with inspiration as I thought back to the conversation I had with Andrea years earlier when she had asked if we could go visit Umuhoza someday. "Sure, Baby. We'll go someday," I had said.

Now I was convinced that our "someday" had arrived.

I went to Darla first. "I'm going to take Andrea to see Umuhoza," I said. "I don't know why exactly, but I think it would do her some good." I was probably thinking that if Andrea could visit Umuhoza in Rwanda and see how most of the world lived, maybe she would better appreciate all that she had and all that she took for granted. Maybe it would be a wake-up call for her, and she would see how fortunate she was.

In hindsight, I was naïve and shortsighted. But even if my motivation had been wrong, the idea ultimately proved to be divinely inspired. God knows why I thought a trip to Rwanda would make a difference, and sure enough, God knew why we needed to go.

I discussed the trip with Darla, and she gave a cautious blessing to the idea. With the two other children and their summer activities, it would be difficult, if not impossible, for the whole family to make the trek, so we decided that I would accompany Andrea to Rwanda alone.

We approached Andrea with the idea, handing her Umuhoza's letter as she was watching TV. "Mom and I have been talking about it," I said, "and we were thinking that maybe it's time I made good on that promise I made to you, that we would go visit her."

Andrea was clearly surprised. "Wait, what? Visit Umuhoza?" she asked, as a hesitant smile spread across her face.

"Yes. I think that after all you have been through—after all *we* have gone through—that it would be a good idea for us to visit her this summer. What do you think?"

"Really?" Andrea said. "I'd love to go!"

I pressed Andrea a bit. "Look, this won't exactly be a vacation. It will take some work to get to Rwanda, and it probably won't be the type of travel and accommodations that we are accustomed to, but after all that you've been through . . ." I paused and corrected myself again. "After all that *we* have been through, I think it may give you an opportunity to learn more about yourself. Maybe give you a fresh perspective on things. Are you good with that?"

"Dad, I really want to go," Andrea said, with what seemed to be genuine excitement in her voice. "I wanted to do something different this summer, and this idea sounds perfect!"

She jumped up off the couch and gave both Darla and me big hugs. It was settled. Andrea was all in, and in just a few short months, she and I would be headed to Rwanda.

Still, there were many variables about the trip and many moving parts to consider, not the least of which was how to get there. Booking a flight was easy, but how would we communicate once we arrived in Rwanda—a country where, at the time, most people did not speak English? How would we find our way around? We knew from Umuhoza's letters that she lived in a village far out in the country. Once outside the capital city, transportation was sure to be a challenge. Most importantly, how would we even find this teenage girl named Umuhoza?

However, I felt that I knew the answer to these issues. "I think I know someone who can help us," I said to Darla.

"Really? Who?"

"I'm going to call William Mwizerwa."

Chapter 8

PRAYERS UNDER FIRE

When my son, Nate, was in first grade, he expressed an interest in joining the Cub Scouts. When we went to sign him up, I met the pack leader and told him my son was eager to be a Tiger Cub in a new den. "Great," the pack leader said. "We just need a dad to volunteer to be the den leader."

No way, I thought, *I've got too much going on*. But as the dozen or so new Tiger Cubs assembled at our table, including some of Nate's first-grade buddies, I knew I couldn't let Nate and his buddies down. So although I went there looking to hand one Tiger Cub off to some other leader, all of the other Tiger Cubs were handed off to me instead.

My approach to our activities was to invite all the dads to the Tiger Cub den meetings so that most projects could be a father/son experience. At our first den meeting of the year, in the fall of 2001, all of the new Tiger Cubs gathered at our house, including David, one of Nate's new friends. David was the youngest of five children in a Rwandan refugee family that had resettled in Brentwood. He was new to Nate's school, and the two of them, having met just weeks earlier, had already become good friends. Like all the new Cubs, David had come to the meeting with his father.

"Hello, I'm Randy Hartley," I said as I introduced myself to David's father.

"Hello, I am William Mwizerwa," he said in a firm, slow tone.

William and I struck up a conversation, and I could instantly tell by his accent that he was not from Nashville. He spoke in slightly broken English, but I was impressed by his quiet confidence. His reserved manner seemed to mask a deep inner strength. He told me that he was from Rwanda.

"Really?" I said. "My family and I have supported a little girl in Rwanda for several years. Her name is Umuhoza."

William responded, "Oh, Umuhoza. That's a good, traditional Rwandan name."

William told me that he worked for African Leadership, a not-for-profit organization that assists in establishing and equipping pastors in Africa. William had started a refugee ministry under the African Leadership umbrella. I could tell right away that William was a man with a strong faith and a strong commitment to his cause. I began to financially support his ministry—but I did not yet know the story of the Mwizerwa family or why that cause was so important to them.

\\\

William and his wife, Ebralie, had grown up with modest means in different parts of rural Rwanda. They each worked hard and were fortunate to grow up as Christians within the Presbyterian Church of Rwanda, best known by its French acronym, EPR or Eglise Presbyterienne au Rwanda. The church played an important role in Rwanda, as it developed an educational system and leadership infrastructure that worked alongside the country's leadership to improve the livelihood of the people. They each attended church school and were baptized there. The opportunity provided by their schooling and their faith would bring their lives together in Kigali, the capital of Rwanda.

In 1975, William accepted his first job in Kigali with the Rwandan National Coffee Company as editor of the company magazine, which educated farmers in Rwanda about growing coffee. As the largest export of the country, coffee was the most important source of foreign currency for the government. In addition to his duties as editor of the company newsletter, William hosted a weekly radio show that encouraged farmers to raise coffee and taught better techniques for raising the most productive crops.

Ebralie studied economics at the Lycee Notre Dame de Citeaux in Kigali, and soon after graduation, she accepted a job with the EPR church offices in Kigali. William's older sister, Zilpa, also worked for EPR, and it was Zilpa that would soon introduce William to Ebralie at the EPR offices in downtown Kigali. The two were married in December 1981.

Devout Christians, William and Ebralie were quite active in their church, and they helped establish other churches in various areas of Kigali, including in Remera-Kicukiro. Members of this church would later start another church in Kanombe, with whom the First Presbyterian Church in Nashville would later develop a close relationship.

By April of 1994, the Mwizerwas had four children, ranging in age from one to eleven, and Ebralie was pregnant with their fifth child. The family was growing, and William and Ebralie were doing well, but little did they know of the tragedy that was about to engulf their entire country.

\\\

There were two major ethnic designations in Rwanda, "Hutu" and "Tutsi." The issues that divided these two groups spanned generations, beginning with colonization by Germany and later Belgium. In the centuries before Europeans arrived, the people who would eventually be designated Hutu were typically farmers, and those labeled Tutsi raised cattle.

Most Rwandans were friendly and kind to one another, despite struggling together to eke out a living. They lived together, spoke the same language, and worshiped the same God; their cultures and customs were identical. The imaginary distinctions created by colonizers were ludicrous, as Rwandans themselves could not tell someone's heritage based only on physical appearances. There were no genetic, historical, or religious differences between the groups, yet the categories imposed by European settlers stuck.

Regardless of historical facts, the political leaders were committed to keeping the nation divided, beginning with the colonizers of the late nineteenth century. By 1935, the Belgian overlords had implemented a national system of identity cards that required every Rwandan to declare his or her ethnicity. These personal ID cards were issued to everyone in the country at age eighteen, with the unmistakable designation of Hutu or Tutsi emblazoned on every card.

The monarch and the administrative positions who served him prior to Belgian colonization happened to be predominately Tutsi, so, unsurprisingly, the Belgians continue to favor this group, giving them administrative power and using them to enforce their rule to make the colony more profitable for Belgium.

Over decades, the resentment of the divisions created by colonial rule built a wall between the Rwandan people and those who benefited from continued colonization. Rwanda remained an impoverished country, and those who were disenfranchised blamed those in administrative positions for their troubles.

In November 1959, turmoil began when the monarch stepped down, and a small minority of Hutus took militant action against Tutsis. Many were killed, and others fled Rwanda to neighboring countries. A Hutu transition government came to power, pushing the divisive issues below the surface for decades. Even though Tutsis were no longer in political power, they continued to be a political scapegoat for issues that faced Rwanda. As issues of poverty and lack of opportunities persisted, the propaganda against the Tutsi minority intensified.

The issues faced by Rwanda—both economic and political—were perpetuated by poor political leadership, with little or no attempt to cultivate an inclusive political establishment or denounce ethnic prejudices. Throughout Rwanda, the citizens suffered from bad economic policies and continued political oppression. The result was violent ethnic bloodlettings that punctuated the next few decades, particularly in 1963 and 1973, which forced many Tutsi families into exile.

Those in exile began to demand a peaceful return to Rwanda, but the Rwandan government was not in favor of their return. Instead, the ruling government said that Rwanda was full, like a glass of water, and had no room for their return. Eventually, the Rwandan Patriotic Front (RPF) was formed, and the RPF began a guerilla war along the northern Rwandan border in 1990 to force the Rwandan ruling party to accept a return of those in exile and to form a new government with a more equitable sharing of power.

After four years of intermittent fighting along the border, and increased ethnic tensions at home, it appeared that a political solution to the issues had been reached. The Rwandan government had agreed to negotiate with the RPF, and after months of difficult negotiations, the terms of a lasting agreement had begun to take shape. The main provisions involved the repatriation of Rwandans in exile and a power-sharing arrangement in the government. It seemed as if both sides of the conflict had made sacrifices and gotten what they wanted—an end to the fighting.

With an outline of an agreement reached, a small force of United Nations peacekeepers and a lightly armed force of 600 RPF fighters were dispatched to Kigali to protect an RPF team of political leaders that were to help implement the terms of the new accord. The pieces were in place, and a final formal regional summit was set to take place in Arusha, Tanzania, where the Arusha Peace Agreement was to be signed. At last, the agreement marked real hope of a new beginning for democracy in Rwanda.

President Juvenal Habyarimana of Rwanda joined a delegation of leaders from around the region in Arusha, Tanzania on April 6, 1994, to sign the historic Arusha Peace Accords. These accords gave hope to the Rwandan people that the fighting would finally end and that there was a framework for lasting peace. Change seemed imminent.

Peace was a real possibility at last, or so the people thought.

This was the situation in which the Mwizerwa family, along with all Rwandans, found themselves as the sun began to set on April 6, 1994.

Chapter 9

HELL'S GATES OPENED

President Habyarimana's Falcon-50 private jet took off at 6:07 p.m. for the short flight from Tanzania to Kigali. President Habyarimana was accompanied by the Burundian president, the Rwandan Army Chief of Staff, six staff members, and three crew members. It was still twilight when the jet entered Rwandan airspace, traveling west on an approach that took it over Kanombe, an area not far from the home of William, Ebralie, and their family.

Just as the plane appeared above the runway, a streak of light burst from the ground toward the aircraft, followed by another flash of light. Though it looked like a shooting star, the light was actually one surface-to-air missile, possibly two. When the missile struck the airplane in flight, the craft exploded and crashed to the earth in a ball of fire as it spread debris all the way to the presidential palace garden, where several large shards of wreckage, a section of the fuselage, and an airplane engine remain to this day. Everyone on board died.

Almost before the plane's wreckage hit the ground, gunfire broke out in Kigali, seemingly everywhere at once. Within a few hours, roadblocks were thrown into place all over Kigali by armed forces and militias comprised of Hutu extremists. Bridges were shut down to both vehicles and pedestrians, as militias and soldiers demanded to examine identity cards before allowing anyone to cross the roadblock.

It seemed odd that the roadblocks and gunfire should ensue so soon after the tragic plane crash. However, a heavy political atmosphere had hung over all peace negotiations. It seemed that each time progress was made, the Hutu extremists within the presidential party and their allies would resort to violence in an effort to end the negotiations. Their property destruction, abuse, and killings had gone on unchecked throughout the process. It appeared as though the sudden explosion of violence after the attack on the president's plane was a well-planned response to the peace accords by the extremists.

Their actions set in motion what a UN special inquiry later called "the systematic slaughter of men, women, and children." The Hutu militia literally began pulling Tutsis out of their cars and shooting them on the spot. Many others were hacked to death with machetes.

The militia's real mission was the extermination of all Tutsis. In a matter of hours, the killings increased exponentially, resulting in the vicious deaths of thousands of Tutsis and of the moderate Hutus who tried to protect them or give them refuge. Violence spread, not merely in the nation's capital, but all over the country, as militias and renegade army units began the planned purging of Rwanda of the Tutsi minority. Totally innocent men, women, and children—people with whom they had sat in the same churches the previous Sunday—were now mortal enemies as the demonic spirits took over the nation.

\\\

William was walking from his office to his home in Kigali, just days before the genocide against Tutsis began, when a young boy said to him that he will be killed anytime. He was stunned and bewildered. There had been ongoing unrest and rumors of greater trouble, but most of the people in Rwanda found such rumors hard to believe.

The Mwizerwa children were playing in the yard with friends on the early evening of April 6 when they suddenly heard a loud explosion, but they had no clue that the president's plane had been the target. Soon, sporadic gunfire crackled in the distance. The sounds grew closer and more persistent. William and Ebralie moved quickly, bringing the children inside, all congregated in the hallway and barricading themselves in their home. In a desperate attempt to keep the stray bullets from coming in the house, they moved furniture and mattresses against the windows.

Trapped in their home, William and Ebralie fielded calls from all over the city, struggling to understand what was happening. By day two, the telephone tower was hit by an explosion, and telephone service was knocked out for all the city, creating a greater sense of isolation and confusion.

Chapter 10

A LOSE-LOSE PROPOSITION

William and Ebralie's oldest daughter was nearly twelve years old at the time of the genocide. "Bullets were flying all over the place outside. Our bedroom was in the front of the house," she later recalled, "where anything could have come through. So we moved whatever we could, including our mattresses, in front of the windows, and we slept in the hallway."

Ebralie remembers, "We prayed and prayed, but nothing stopped." Indeed, the senseless killing continued unabated throughout the night. Gunshots frequently punctured the dark night as the Mwizerwa family huddled closely together in the hallway, praying and trying to sleep.

After two days of hiding in their home, William and Ebralie

heard loud pounding on their front door. Instinctively, Ebralie tugged the children to her body, as though shielding them from the sounds and whatever they represented. The loud thumping on the door continued.

"William!" a loud male voice called. "Ebralie! Are you in there?"

William breathed a sigh of relief. "It's Hein," he said to Ebralie and the children. Hein was a German missionary from Wuppertal sent by Vereinte Evangelische Mission (VEM), a partner of the Rwandan Protestant Council. He lived nearby and worked closely with Ebralie at the council.

Hein had come to tell William and Ebralie that all German nationals were being pulled out of Rwanda. The situation was bleak, and he was deeply worried about what would happen to the Mwizerwas. He brought all the food and drink that he had from his home, hoping against hope that the provisions would help sustain the family long enough for conditions to improve.

Then in a magnanimous gesture of concern and compassion, Hein made an offer. "I want to take at least one member of your family to safety," he said. "You probably won't make it. They want to kill you. So let me take your youngest child, and I will raise him as my own." Hein strongly believed that the rest of the family would be killed, but hoped that if he took the one-year-old boy, at least he would have a chance to live.

William and Ebralie quickly thought and prayed over their few options. But in the end, Ebralie told Hein, "This child is not on your passport. You will get to the first roadblock, and they will kill the baby, cut him in half, and you will not forgive yourself." Ebralie assured Hein that God would protect them. Hein nodded in agreement with Ebralie, and then prayed with the family before leaving.

Not knowing how long he would be gone, Hein gave some money to his night watchman to pass on to the Mwizerwas, so that they could pay his staff for a period of time. Hein also had a microphone that he had repaired for William, which William used for his weekly radio show. Hein asked the night watchmen to return the microphone to William when he delivered the money.

As the watchman made his way to the Mwizerwa's to deliver the items, he was stopped and searched by government soldiers on patrol. The soldiers found the money from Hein in an envelope, along with the microphone, which raised their suspicions. The next day, the soldiers along with militiamen arrived at the Mwizerwa's home, and ordered William and Ebralie to lay in the street as they were questioned about the items.

The militia was convinced that the microphone and money were somehow connected to the contingent of RPF soldiers that were stationed at the parliament building on the hillside opposite the Mwizerwa home, and accused William of communicating with the enemy. As William was pleading his case, there was loud explosion just yards away.

Following the explosion, the militiamen ran up the street and began exchanging gunfire with the RFP soldiers from across the hill. After hours of fighting, the Mwizerwas finally made their way back into their home and prayed continually through the night. Fortunately for them, the militia did not return.

\\\

In all prior outbreaks of ethnic violence in Rwanda, those who were able to make it to a church were spared since the militias normally did not violate the sanctity of these holy spaces. Consequently, when this round of violence exploded, many thousands of Rwandans made their way to houses of worship, thinking they would find refuge from the evil that had engulfed their land. Instead, in many cases, they had unwittingly run directly into death traps.

In Nyamata Catholic Church, for example, located about twenty miles south of Kigali, more than 10,000 frightened Rwandans had gathered on the grounds by April 10, seeking shelter from the Interahamwe militias. But shelter was nowhere to be found: the Interahamwe used grenades to blow open the heavy steel gate, and the hordes of militiamen unleashed unspeakable atrocities on those in the church. Some were killed or maimed by grenades thrown into the crowds. Some of the victims were slaughtered at the altar like perverse sacrifices. Many were mangled by the sharp-edged machetes, knives, and clubs swung madly, as though in a demonically inspired rage. The brutality knew no limits. Bodies piled on top of one another, on top of the pews, between the pews, and on the ground. Many women were repeatedly raped and beaten before they were hacked to death.[1] Blood soon stained the cement floors and even the brick walls of the church.

More than eight hundred thousand people—men, women, and children—were senselessly slaughtered during one hundred days and nights of terror. Ebralie remembers, "At night, we heard the gunshots around the house. Each time the telephone rang, someone asked, 'Are you still alive? So and so is dead.' We realized that people were dying all around us."

William and Ebralie gathered their children together. They prayed and read Psalm 23: "The Lord is my shepherd. … Though I walk through the valley of the shadow of death, I will fear no evil."

Afterward, they told the children, "Prepare yourself. You may die at any minute now."

It is impossible to imagine the emotions of anyone trying to navigate through the terror of those days, but it is particularly difficult to understand how those emotions would impact the children who one day were playing in their yard; the next day they were waiting for their turn to die.

Chapter 11

SEPARATED
BY HOPE

After holding out at home for the first few days of terror, William realized that it was just a matter of time before they were discovered. He realized that his family needed to leave. The day after the encounter with the militia, the Mwizerwa family saw thousands of people from their neighborhood running for the Kicukiro school complex, which was up the street from their home. The United Nations had a contingent of Belgian soldiers stationed at the school complex on a hill overlooking their neighborhood, a relatively short walk from their home. The presence of the Belgian troops had protected those seeking refuge from the ever-present militias.

William and Ebralie made the decision to join their neighbors at the Kicukiro school, but as the family prepared to leave, one of the strongest storms of the rainy season pelted the area around Kigali. William and Ebralie nervously surveyed the scene, trying to decide whether they should proceed with their plans. They hoped to wait out the weather, but the torrential downpour continued incessantly.

William finally made a decision. Ebralie had already been weak and ill with her pregnancy, and William feared that the cold, driving rain would make matters worse. The conditions would be difficult for the other young children as well. Furthermore, there was no guarantee that they would safely make it to the school.

With no small measure of trepidation, the Mwizerwas decided to sequester where they were. The family locked down tightly again, praying through another day as they attempted to avoid the evil chaos that had enveloped Rwanda.

Little did William know that at the time of his decision, the UN had ordered the small remaining contingent of Belgian soldiers to abandon the school. As the soldiers pulled out, some of the thousands of those gathered there tried to follow or climb aboard the vehicles, but the soldiers pushed them off and fired into the air, leaving those who were desperate for their protection at the mercy of the militias.

In the end, the nearly five thousand people who had sought protection from the UN at the school compound were slaughtered instead. Only an estimated one hundred people survived, most of them buried under the piles of bodies of people who died from the grenades, gunshots, and machete attacks.

\\\

The sun had barely risen over the picturesque ridges and valleys of

Kigali when William and his family made the difficult decision to escape the city and find refuge elsewhere. As the family left behind the horrors that they had seen, they had no idea what may lie in front of them.

The Mwizerwa family inched along toward the border and out of Rwanda. Narrowly escaping death several times, they knew angels surrounded them, and they found God's favor at every turn. Most people they encountered showed great mercy, though on occasion William used what money they had to "buy their lives," paying off would-be attackers whenever they encountered trouble along the way. Thankfully, they also encountered many Rwandans who risked their lives to assist them and others who were simply trying to escape the hell that had taken over their country.

The Mwizerwa family eventually made it to Kenya, but the maniacal killing continued back home, exacerbated by the retreat of the United Nations "peacekeeping" forces that had been stationed in Rwanda. The United Nations Security Council voted to withdraw most of its peacekeeping operation (UNAMIR). Even the troops that remained were not authorized to act, opening the door to further killing. European nations stood by without engaging, and the U.S. was reluctant to get involved, at least partially because the images of eighteen American Rangers killed in Somalia during the Black Hawk Down incident in Mogadishu still haunted leaders.[2] Consequently, most Americans were ignorant of the horrendous suffering of the Rwandan people until after the genocide had subsided.

The killing only stopped after the RPF defeated their government army and extremist counterparts. It took the RPF led by Paul Kagame three full months to push the government and militias to the south of Rwanda. By then, nearly a million Tutsis and moderate

Hutus were dead. Too little, too late, the French initiative, named Operation Turquoise, was launched with the intent to establish a "humanitarian protection zone" in southwestern Rwanda, which separated the warring factions.

When the violence finally ended in July 1994, the country faced enormous obstacles to recovery. Of the country's eight million residents, more than eight hundred thousand men, women, and children had been slaughtered. Millions of others had been displaced. The government and business structures were in shambles.

The Mwizerwa family eventually made their way to Nairobi, Kenya, where friends helped them in getting settled in a small apartment. The family members all felt fear, anger, and shame knowing what Rwanda had been through and what the people had done to each other. They quickly began to learn a new language and a new culture as they started their new life.

The family adapted to life in Kenya as best they could, not knowing that this would be their home for the next few years. Ebralie gave birth to their fifth child, David, three months after their arrival in Kenya. The older children enrolled in school, and Ebralie and William took undergraduate classes at Daystar University.

William and Ebralie had a family friend who had left Rwanda before the genocide and settled in Nashville, Tennessee. The friend had met a church missionary, Deborah Martin, who was home in Nashville on vacation from her work at the Kakuma refugee camp in Kenya. The friend asked if Deborah would check on the Mwizerwa family when she returned to Kenya, and pass along a gift.

The Mwizerwa family received a call from Deborah when she returned to Kenya, and soon Deborah met with William and Ebralie. She learned about the family and their situation before returning to her work at Kakuma.

A few months later, William began working with U.S. Embassy personnel on his case. They told him that, while there were no guarantees, it may be possible for William to obtain a temporary visa, which would allow him to travel to the United States and remain in the country while his case for asylum was heard.

When William was finally told that his application for a temporary visa was approved, he was conflicted; the opportunity was bittersweet. On the one hand, it provided William a chance to move to America to start a new life. On the other hand, his family would not immediately be eligible to accompany him. In fact, it was unclear when, if ever, they would be able to join him. William prayed and fasted for seven days, seeking direction and asking God for guidance regarding this decision. Ultimately, William called his friend Hein, the German who had been his neighbor in Kigali, to ask for advice. Hein told William that he would buy him a round-trip ticket. Hein promised that if William did not like America, he could return to his family in Kenya.

As William weighed Hein's offer, he felt trepidation. Most of what he knew about America had come from old Westerns and gangster films, where it appeared as though violence was rampant across the country. Having recently escaped the genocide, the last thing William wanted was a return to violence. William also wondered if he would be able to find a good church home in America, as the Hollywood perspective did not make America appear welcoming to Christians. However, William was familiar with Billy Graham from his crusades throughout Rwanda in the 1970s, and that gave him hope.

In 1998, William made the decision to take advantage of his

opportunity and head to America—alone. With little more than a visa, the phone number of his friend in Nashville, and the clothes on his back, William Mwizerwa boarded a plane to Tennessee.

As he said his goodbyes and hugged each family member, he had no idea how long it would be until he saw them again. Boarding that plane would be a test of faith, even for someone with as strong of faith as William. As it turned out, it would be almost exactly two years and nine months—one thousand days—before William would be able to hold his wife and five children again.

Chapter 12

STARTING OVER

After more than thirty hours of airplane flights and layovers, William looked out the window of the aircraft as it approached the airport in Nashville, Tennessee. This would be William's new home going forward—a home without family for the first time in his life, but a home with hope for the first time in four years.

When William arrived in Nashville, his friend from Rwanda offered to let him stay with him and his family as William got settled. While it was nice to have people who could understand his experience and speak his language, William quickly realized that staying in the small home with a family of five was not going to work. Thankfully for William, God had an answer for his dilemma.

Just a couple of days after arriving in Nashville, William was at a grocery store when he ran into Deborah Martin. She was again home on vacation from her work at the Kakuma refugee camp, and just happened to be at the store when she saw William. As they talked, William mentioned that he was looking for a church home. Deborah recalled that William was Presbyterian, so she gave him the contact information for First Presbyterian Church of Nashville.

That Friday afternoon, William called the church and soon was talking to Pastor John Crawford, and the following Monday, William met with Pastor Crawford at the church. After learning about William's situation, John was struck by what he had heard—not only because of William's plight, but also by how the church might be in a perfect position to help.

"William, I think our church might have just what you need," the pastor said with a smile. He led William across the church grounds to an empty parsonage on the edge of the property. "The parsonage here at the church is available," John said. "You can stay here at no cost as long as you'd like until God provides you with another home." With that, John handed William the keys.

William could hardly believe what the pastor was offering him, but he was grateful for God's provision. "Oh my! What a blessing. I am so thankful to you and to the church. Are you sure?"

"Absolutely," John replied. "We are happy that God has provided this opportunity for us to help you at just the right time."

"Amen!" William said with a broad smile. Ironically, one of William's fears in coming to America was that he would not be able to find a church home, a congregation with whom he would be comfortable worshiping. Now he had been given a church *home*—quite literally—within days of his arrival in Nashville.

The First Presbyterian Church of Nashville would continue to bless the Mwizerwas in the months and years to come. One member, Don Albright, met William at the church shortly after he first arrived. After hearing about William's background, Don astutely realized that William had next to nothing materially.

"What do you need?" he asked William when they met. "What can I do for you?"

William could have asked Don for material things, and no doubt Don would have done his best to supply William's needs, but William only asked for one thing: "I need someone to be a prayer partner," he told a shocked Don. So they prayed together that day, and Don and William have been meeting and praying together weekly ever since.

Don Albright and his family became an important part of William's life. Through them, William learned many things about life in America, and the Albright family was able to learn about life and culture in Rwanda. For William's first Christmas in America, the Albrights invited William over to celebrate, and the family sang carols around the piano. William was surprised to hear tunes he had learned as a young boy, but the language of the songs was different. So the Albrights taught William the carols in English, and William taught them to the Albrights in Kinyarwanda. On this and many other occasions, they all saw how God worked through them, and how He used their prayer time especially. They both felt God speaking to them in those times of prayer, and could see God fulfilling His promises.

Don was a Sunday school teacher and introduced William to the class he led at First Presbyterian Church. The class adopted William as one of their own, and prayed faithfully for William and his family. They especially prayed that the family would soon be reunited. Don and the First Presbyterian Church family were quite a blessing to

William, one for which he is eternally grateful. William would later say that he could never repay Don for his love and patience.

When William first arrived in Nashville, he was not able to legally work since he had not yet obtained a work permit. Instead, he helped a friend he had met at church who had a pool-cleaning business. William didn't mind not getting paid—he just wanted to meet people and work on learning a new language. William was already fluent in four languages, but now in his forties, he was learning his fifth—English!

William also volunteered to help the church youth soccer team. Soccer was very popular in Rwanda, and William loved to play, but he especially loved learning English from the children. William noticed that adults were reluctant or embarrassed to say anything about his fractured English, but the children were quick to correct him. If William said something wrong, they cheerfully let him know, "We don't say it that way!" William credited those children for being his best English tutors.

After William obtained a work permit, his first paying job was sewing mattresses at the Jamison Bedding Company in Nashville. He was glad to be working, both to earn a living and to help pass the days. As he became more connected to the church, and as more people began to know of him, William learned of communities of refugees and immigrants in Nashville who were going through similar experiences. He was soon organizing a Christian fellowship with them and working with hundreds, helping them manage the newness of American life—just as he had done. So while Jamison Bedding Company provided his employment, helping other refugees became his passion.

\\\

When William left for America, he and Ebralie had made a commitment to write a letter to each other every day. At that time, there was no widespread Internet, and international phone calls were terribly expensive. So for the next one thousand days, they faithfully wrote to each other, hoping and praying that they could be together again. Ebralie would later say how much she cherished those letters, saving them to read and reread again and again because they were so sweet and she missed William so much. Little did she know that her collection of letters would one day prove to be invaluable.

Back in Kenya, Ebralie was slogging through the painstakingly slow immigration process and attempting to secure a visa for herself and for the children. Her situation of missing her husband while trying to stay strong for the family in their new home in Kenya was difficult enough, but adding to the emotional stress was the fact that there appeared to be no timetable for the end of her separation from William. Ebralie dealt with ongoing delays for nearly two and a half years as one government official after another raised obstacles related to the family's immigration process.

Ebralie faithfully completed all of the required forms, carefully answering the many questions to the best of her ability and dealing with the incessant red tape. At last, she put on her Sunday-best dress and took all of the paperwork to the immigration office in Nairobi.

The small office was staffed by only a few workers, and the waiting room was crowded with people hoping to be granted travel visas. A heavyset African woman in an official looking uniform sat behind a desk that was stacked high with papers and forms. The woman scowled as she reviewed Ebralie's visa request.

After a few minutes, she reached to the side of her stack of papers, picked up a large ink stamp, and slammed it down on Ebralie's information packet, leaving a red-inked impression on the top paper: DENIED.

"Denied?" Ebralie asked.

"That's what it says," the woman behind the desk replied curtly, her no-nonsense tone implying that her decision was final.

"But why?" Ebralie asked, tears forming in her eyes.

The immigration official noticed Ebralie's tears and softened slightly. "Woman, I see this every day," she said. "A man abandons his family, starts a new life somewhere else, and the family is left here without a clue."

"My husband would not abandon us," Ebralie protested. "He would never do that. He is an honorable man!"

Despite her insistence, the immigration official was unmoved. "The story of your husband in America sounds good—but you need proof!"

Ebralie was discouraged by the constant delays, but she never gave up on getting approval for the visas. Then one day, as Ebralie was reading her daily letter from William, it suddenly dawned on her that she had the proof she needed right in her hand. She put the letter in the box that contained every single letter that William had sent to her from America, and then she took the box with her to the immigration office in Nairobi. The same woman sat behind the desk.

When Ebralie's name was called, she boldly stepped inside the office and said, "You asked me for proof that this man still loves me. Here it is." Ebralie then slowly spilled the entire box full of letters across the immigration officer's desk.

"Here is my proof. My husband has not abandoned us," Ebralie smiled. "He still loves me."

The caustic immigration official picked up a few of the letters, slowly examining each one. She noticed that each letter was hand-written—not typed—and every letter was in the same handwriting—William's. After thumbing through several of the letters, the amazed immigration officer looked up at Ebralie with a hint of a tear in her eye. "This man loves you, for sure."

"I knew that!" Ebralie gushed.

"You need to go," the immigration officer said. She reached past the pile of papers on her desk and grabbed a large blue ink stamp. She slammed the stamp down on the top page of Ebralie's application: APPROVED.

Outside the office, Ebralie and the children could barely contain themselves as they thanked and praised God. She and her children were going to join William in America! After one thousand days apart, the Mwizerwa family would be together again! Their prayers had been answered, and their faith had been rewarded.

Years later, long after the family had been reunited in Nashville, William and Ebralie chose a few special letters from all those they had saved. They framed the letters and gave one to each of their children as a reminder of those times. The letters also provide a powerful testimony that love was able to keep the family united, even while they were thousands of miles apart.

Chapter 13

UNLIKELY PARTNERS

William, along with a large group of supporters from First Presbyterian Church, waited at the Nashville airport to welcome Ebralie and the children. They watched anxiously as passengers exited from the concourse leading to the baggage area. Oblivious to the crowd, William peered into the waves of people flowing in his direction. Finally, the face William had yearned to see for the last thousand days appeared: Ebralie, with their five children in tow. She was here! They were reunited! For the first time in almost three years, the Mwizerwa family would share a home and country once more. William ran to his wife and embraced her, and then he gathered each of his children, one by one, into his open arms.

As they hugged, the awaiting crowd burst into a song of celebration, and Pastor John Tyndall led the crowd in a prayer of thanksgiving, right there in the lobby of the airport. William's new church family shared in the sheer joy of witnessing a father seeing his wife and children after being apart for so long—and the relief of a mother who knew that her family was finally together again after the many months and years of not knowing what would happen. William and Ebralie would finally be able to build a life in this new and unfamiliar land, and they would be able to do so with the familiar love and comfort of a family.

Much had changed in the almost three years that had passed. The whole family had grown. William's youngest sons who were only three and four years old when William left for America. What a journey the family had been on for the past seven years! They had survived the genocide, left Rwanda for Kenya, and William had gone to America—but now the whole family was finally back together again.

Just as He had done for William, God continued to open doors for the Mwizerwa family. Brentwood Academy, a private Christian school just south of Nashville, accepted the three older children for admission. Not only did it provide an excellent educational opportunity, but it also provided an amazing start for their children in being incorporated to life in America. The school staff, students, and parents helped the healing of the children, and their adaptation to a new culture and a new community.

Not long after the whole Mwizerwa family arrived in Nashville, they faced another dilemma. First Presbyterian Church had been quite generous to allow the family to live in the church parsonage while they got settled, but due to changes in the church staff, the church leaders informed William that the church needed the parsonage. The family would need to find a new place to live soon.

William and Ebralie had no idea where to go, but they continued to faithfully pray for God's direction and provision, willing to go wherever He would lead them. Brentwood Academy invited the family to share their testimony at a school assembly. As part of the assembly, students performed a sketch on peace and reconciliation, and parents were invited to attend. In the audience that day seated next to Ebralie were Lisa and Doug Durr, who were the parents of a student at the school. Lisa and Doug were so moved by what they had heard that, afterwards, Lisa approached William and Ebralie and asked if they could help them in any way. What did they need?

Perhaps it was because of the cultural differences at the time, or perhaps it was because of the desperation that Ebralie felt to find her family a new home, but in an uncharacteristic moment for the selfless Ebralie, she quickly replied to Lisa, "We need a home to live in."

What Ebralie could not have known at the time was that Doug and Lisa Durr had just finished building a new home that happened to be right behind our house in Brentwood. Doug and Lisa were ready to move from the more modest, temporary housing down the street where they had been living, and they had just been talking about what they might want to do with the now-empty space. A day after that conversation, they met a family of refugees in need of a place to stay. Immediately, the Durrs knew that God had called them to make their prior house a home for the Mwizerwas.

It was that providential twist that brought the Mwizerwa family to Brentwood, Tennessee, at the start of the 2001 school year. Their youngest son, David, would enroll in first grade at Scales Elementary School, where he would become friends with my son, Nate. David joined my Cub Scout den, and I then met William Mwizerwa. God was truly working in mysterious ways, and the threads of our lives were just beginning to be sewn together in God's divine tapestry.

Of course, I did not know what the future held when William showed up with his son at the Cub Scout meeting in Brentwood in 2001. We saw each other regularly at our sons' meetings, and although I really didn't know William's background, it was easy to see that he had a heart to help people—forged out of his own pain. As I talked more with him, he told me that he was working with refugees under the African Leadership umbrella.

The initial group he had been helping were some of the "Lost Boys" of Sudan. Now young men, they had been orphaned as boys during the war in South Sudan. Many of their friends and siblings died during their horrific journey out of Sudan to refugee camps in Ethiopia and Kenya.

During the Christmas holidays in 2000, William was having dinner with his family when he received a call from Deborah Martin, the missionary worker who met William in Kenya. She was calling to tell William that four young adults from Sudan had literally been dropped off in Nashville with no money, no jobs, and little understanding of the language and culture. She asked if there was anything that William could do to help.

William had his hands full raising his own five children, but he couldn't help but wonder, "If those were my children, and something happened to me, I would hope that somebody would provide a father figure for them." So that's what he did. Before long, he was mentoring those four from Sudan, then ten, then eventually one hundred and fifty. With the help of many volunteers who offered to help, they started by teaching them English, helped them get into school, and taught them how to fill out job applications. Over time, one hundred and twenty-three of the initial one hundred and fifty Lost Boys not only graduated from high school, but went on to graduate from college.

As William's services expanded to hundreds and hundreds of refugees, he sensed that he needed to move his refugee ministry out from under the umbrella of African Leadership. William and Ebralie prayed and fasted for a weekend, asking for God's direction and vision for their new ministry. It was over that weekend that they were led to move their refugee ministry and start Legacy Mission Village (LMV).

William invited several people who had been supporting him in his efforts, including me, his prayer partner Don Albright, Doug and Lisa Durr, and some other members of First Presbyterian Church to serve on his board of directors. In our first meeting, William told us that he and Ebralie both felt that it was their legacy to serve others. "We should have died several times in 1994," he said, "but God spared our lives. We feel that the time we have left here on Earth is a loan from God, and we want to spend the rest of our days repaying that loan." *What a beautiful and heartfelt way of viewing life*, I thought.

Legacy Mission Village has since served thousands and thousands of refugees. LMV truly meets the entire spectrum of needs for refugee families, including providing assistance in resettlement, helping with housing and employment, tutoring students and preparing younger kids for school, helping with citizenship, and providing ESL (English as a Second Language) classes for adults. And of course, under the leadership of William as the executive director, LMV knows exactly what those needs are. It has been amazing to see the tireless work that William and his whole family put into their calling.

In the refugee community in Nashville today, he is simply known as "Mr. William." Whether the refugees are from Congo, Burundi,

Nepal, Myanmar, Syria, or Iraq, William and LMV serve them all
with the same compassion, grace, and love of Jesus. William's reputation has grown. On one occasion, a refugee had flown into Nashville,
just as William had done years earlier. Lost and confused upon landing in America, the refugee looked to the airport officials for help, but
he could only say two words in English: "Mr. William." Thankfully,
the airport officials knew just who to call, and "Mr. William" immediately came to assist the newly arrived refugee, just as he has done
so many other times over the years.

\\\

I knew almost none of this when I contacted William to see if
he could help guide Andrea and me to Rwanda in 2009 to meet
Umuhoza. Sure, I had gotten to know William a little, and our sons,
Nate and David, had become friends. William had invited Darla and
me to attend a few fundraising events, and we were glad to support
his work. But from 2001 to 2009, I knew William primarily as a
parent of one of my son's friends.

As Andrea neared the end of her junior year in high school, I
reached out to William. "William, I'd like to take my daughter to
Rwanda to meet Umuhoza, the young lady with whom my daughter
has been exchanging letters for several years. I think it might help
Andrea. Would you be able to join us on a trip to Rwanda this summer? I'd cover your expenses if you could come along with us."

"I will not be able to go," William told me straightforwardly, "but
Ebralie is planning a mission trip to Rwanda through The Outreach
Foundation of the Presbyterian Church."

"Really?" I asked. "If I pay for Ebralie's flights, would she be willing to travel with Andrea and me in advance of her mission trip, helping with translation and getting where we need to go?"

William didn't answer right away. He simply paused before he said, "Let's ask her."

William called me back a day or two later and said that they thought Ebralie would be able to accompany us to Rwanda. He suggested that I meet with him and Ebralie to discuss the trip to make sure we all had the same expectations and to confirm the plans.

At the time of my call to William, I had not yet met Ebralie. So it was with a bit of nervous excitement that I met with William and Ebralie to discuss our trip.

I was immediately taken by Ebralie's bubbly personality and infectious smile. She was a great complement to the quiet and reserved nature of William. After exchanging pleasantries, I told her a bit about Umuhoza and our plans to go and meet her. I also explained how I wanted Andrea to volunteer with the children at Legacy Mission Village so that she would have a greater appreciation for our journey. I didn't tell her yet about all the issues we had with Andrea, other than to say that I thought the trip would be good for her.

Ebralie was wonderful. She worked for the Outreach Foundation of the Presbyterian church, so she had quite a bit of experience with mission trips. She gave great advice for maximizing the value and benefit of our upcoming trip, and I appreciated the passion that Ebralie shared with William in serving others.

It was agreed that the timing for the trip would work and that Ebralie would serve as our guide in Rwanda. I knew I would be grateful for the help, but I did not realize at the time what an amazing blessing it would be for Andrea and me to have Ebralie with us—the first of countless blessings we were to receive.

\\\

With our plans for the trip now firmly established, there was one more piece of the puzzle that needed to fall into place.

I went back to Andrea and told her that we were going to be able to make this trip happen. "But," I said, "you are going to have to pay for your trip."

"Dad, how can I do that? I don't even have a job, and I sure don't have any money."

"The way you will pay for the trip," I said, "is to volunteer at Legacy Mission Village. If you volunteer every week, I'll credit that toward the trip. Besides, working with the refugees will give you a better understanding of Umuhoza and the people we will meet."

"Okay," she said hesitantly. "I can do that, I think."

Andrea had heard of Legacy Mission Village. She was aware of William and Ebralie, and she knew David through Nate, but she did not know much more about it. She was not necessarily ecstatic about the idea of volunteering her time at Legacy Mission Village, but she didn't seem opposed to it either. Her volunteer responsibilities would primarily involve tutoring the refugee children who were between the ages of six and twelve, and perhaps playing with them during their breaks.

We set up Andrea's first volunteer session to begin after school one day. She was met there by William and his oldest daughter, Aimee, who also worked for LMV. She had experience with kids who had grown up in the "Brentwood Bubble," the protective cocoon of affluence for which we were grateful, but which many of Andrea's friends and classmates took for granted. Aimee had seen them before—the Brentwood kids who showed up to work at LMV merely to meet their school's public service requirements. They would serve, meet the requirements, and never come back.

"They don't really care about the ministry," Aimee observed. "They just want to get their community service hours and go." Aimee would assign tasks, oversee the volunteers, and wait to see their level of engagement. She did not treat Andrea differently, even though she knew of our family connections.

On her first day, Andrea jumped right into the middle of a bunch of young Burundian children playing out on the playground, and the kids instantly swarmed her, hugging her and laughing.

For Andrea, who had wallowed in deep feelings of low self-esteem and worthlessness for most of her teenage years, the response of the refugee children to her presence immediately melted her heart. It was as though those innocent children were able to peel away the layers of guilt and shame that had built up around her. Those children weren't judging Andrea for where she had been or what she had done. They, too, had all been wounded through the trauma of their refugee journey, and in some way that seemed to bond them.

Volunteering with the refugee children helped improve Andrea's behavior issues more than anything else we had done. Something about getting her eyes off herself and helping others who could do nothing for her in return helped reset Andrea's heart. As Ebralie often said, "Helping others is the best way to heal"—and Andrea was healing. Something happened within her as she volunteered at Legacy Mission Village.

Andrea would later explain her thoughts to us. "How could I be worthless if those little kids couldn't wait to see me show up—when those kids looked forward so much to seeing me every day?" she said.

For the remainder of her junior year, she volunteered twice a week to tutor children in the program. Often, Andrea was there long after the other volunteers had left the premises. After a while, Aimee noticed and soon she saw that there was something special about Andrea. "She was different. She kept coming, day after day," said Aimee. "I could tell there was something different with Andrea, and so could the kids."

William also noticed. He knew that she would be going to Rwanda that summer, so maybe that made some difference, but it seemed to be more than that. William noted, "Even when the after-school program was finished and we sent the children out and the volunteers home, Andrea would stay and play with the children. Sometimes a couple of hours later, I would go to leave the office, and I would find Andrea still playing with the kids on the playground. I would have to say to her, 'Andrea, it is time to go home. You need to go home and eat.'"

Although I didn't know it at the time, as Andrea served those young children, the transformation I was hoping for had already begun. Andrea finally seemed to be emerging from the dark cloud under which she had been living for several years—but we weren't home free yet.

Chapter 14

NOT THERE YET

I couldn't have been more pleased with how things were progressing for our upcoming trip. The fact that Ebralie would travel with us and serve as our guide gave us a great feeling of comfort, and Andrea's volunteering at Legacy Mission Village had proved far more beneficial than anyone could have hoped. Her attitude had changed so much for the better. She was happy again! That precocious young girl who could light up a room with her wit was back, and it was so great to have her home. Our family life had really settled down, and it felt as though our home was back in order. *I can finally relax*, I thought. All the details had been worked out and the arrangements had been made. Soon Andrea and I would be on our way to Africa.

One June evening, just a couple of weeks before the trip, Darla and I were at home watching television when the phone rang. "Mr. Hartley, this is Officer Jones of the Franklin Police Department. We have arrested your daughter and have her here in the Williamson County jail on a drug charge."

"What?" I said. "Is this a joke? You've got to be kidding."

"No, sir," the officer said. "I am not joking. I wish I was."

Shell-shocked by the news, Darla and I quickly made the ten-mile drive to downtown Franklin to bail Andrea out from jail.

"Dad, it is not what it seems," Andrea said as soon as she saw me. "I didn't do anything, and I'm not doing drugs. I was anxious, and I just wanted something to calm me on the plane. I didn't know we were going to a drug dealer's place."

"Andrea," I said, barely maintaining my composure, "how could you do this? How could you not use better sense?"

Once again, just as our hopes had been pumped up and we believed that Andrea was making great progress, we had another setback. Darla and I drove her home that night in silence. When we got back to the house, Andrea rushed inside in a huff.

At that moment, I was beyond exasperated. How could we be going through this again? After everything we had been through, after all of the progress made—and then this! Andrea insisted that it was all just an innocent mistake, but my wounds were too fresh to fully believe it. It was only when Andrea realized that her trip to Rwanda was in jeopardy that she fully understood the gravity of the situation.

I hired an attorney, and we met with him. Andrea insisted that she really was innocent. She said that she had simply told a friend she was really nervous about flying, and the friend said that she knew some-thing that could solve that problem. The two of them took off in the friend's car and drove to a motel room in Franklin. Andrea insisted that she did not know that anything was amiss, but when the two of them went into the room, they were quickly followed by the police on a sting operation. Everyone in the room was arrested.

The lawyer explained that the police found drugs and drug paraphernalia in the hotel room, and since no one claimed them, the charges were levied against everyone in the room. No matter how innocent Andrea thought she was, Tennessee law said that she was guilty.

At that point, everything was thrown into limbo. We were uncertain whether we were going to be able to travel to Rwanda or not. Andrea's future court dates might conflict with our travel plans, and any court restrictions could prevent Andrea from going; so much depended on Andrea's preliminary court hearing. As had been the case for much of the past few years, it felt like my feelings were on a yo-yo. I had been so hopeful that our planned trip to Rwanda might help break this cycle of emotional ups and downs and would finally put Andrea on a firm path to full recovery. And then to be blindsided by this? The entire plan depended on the outcome of Andrea's case. Fortunately, her initial hearing came up quickly.

Although Andrea was a juvenile, she was charged along with the rest of the people in the hotel room whom the police had rounded up that night. Because it was Andrea's first offense, our attorney suggested that Andrea plead guilty, hoping that with good behavior, the charge could be expunged from her record after a year or two. As we huddled with the attorney, we resigned ourselves to that plan.

The eighteen-year-old who had rented the room and was selling the drugs, however, was an adult. The day before Andrea's court appearance, that teen was brought into court. He pled guilty, admitting that he, and no one else, was the one who had attempted to sell the narcotics. "Dad," Andrea asked after a friend texted her the news, "do you think this will make a difference?"

"I don't know, Andrea," I answered somberly. "I'd certainly hope so, but we won't know for sure."

When we went into court the next morning, we brought that information to the judge's attention. After a brief recess to check on the adult drug dealer's charges, the judge concurred. The charges against Andrea should be dropped.

Nevertheless, the judge spoke candidly to Andrea. "Alright, young lady. You are lucky," he said firmly. "You are off the hook this time. But if you continue down this path, you will be back in here. You won't be so lucky then."

Andrea said nothing but nodded in understanding.

Her arrest was another heartrending incident in the continuing cycle of issues that reminded Darla and me that we were not yet where we wanted to be with Andrea. In fact, it seemed that every time we felt that Andrea was making progress and we thought we could breathe again, she would suddenly experience another setback.

But the trip to Rwanda was back on, and that is what mattered at the moment. We packed our bags and prepared to travel halfway around the world to meet another teenage girl who had experienced a much different sort of nightmare.

Chapter 15

MORE THAN AN ADVENTURE

Andrea had been a "Daddy's girl" during her first twelve years of life, but in living through the nightmare of the past few years, our relationship had been strained. I was praying that the trip might help Andrea and me to build—or revive—a special connection. Darla and I hoped that this experience would stimulate a fresh start for all of us, but especially for our daughter.

On July 9, the day before we were to leave Nashville and fly out to Rwanda, I mulled over those thoughts in my mind. I wanted to set the tone for the trip. We were only five months removed from rehab, and just a week past Andrea's court date when I had not even been sure we would be able to go to Rwanda—so my heart and mind were torn. Would this trip be a waste of time, or could it be transformational? I just didn't know.

I went upstairs, sat down at a computer, and began typing a letter to Andrea. I had no preconceived notions about what I should write or how Andrea would respond to my thoughts about what to expect from our trip. As much as I loved Andrea, my relationship with her had been rocky for the past eighteen months or more, and I thought it might be easier for me to write about my hopes for our trip rather than trying to engage her in a conversation about them. So I simply wrote to her from my heart.

It was not a meticulously crafted letter, nor was it a contrived message through which I was purposely trying to manipulate her. It was more like, "These things are on my heart and mind, and I want to share them with you now while they are bursting within me." So I wrote:

> Dear Andrea,
>
> I am excited to be going on this adventure with you. I hope that it is coming at a good time. You are a bright, beautiful, fun-loving, caring young lady. I love you so much! I have to say, though, that for the life of me I cannot understand the decisions you make sometimes. Your decisions not only harm you, but they harm your friends, your family, and your relationships. You know our family has been through quite a bit in the last year. Every time I start to relax and think things will be fine, it seems we have to reopen

old scars.

I pray daily that you are happy and healthy. I pray daily that you are making the right decisions. You have such a great future and opportunity in front of you. Unfortunately, bad decisions dim those opportunities. Young people never seem to grasp the big picture, so us old men try to do that for you.

This African adventure will give you a great opportunity to reflect. Reflect upon your life, your goals, your dream, maybe even your purpose. The Brentwood Bubble will be burst, and you will see what the majority of the world is like. I hope you (we!) will see God at work and learn more about how He can work in us and through us. If we really try to stop, look, listen, and pay attention to what God can show us on this trip, it will make us better people and lead us to make better, smarter decisions.

I paused for a few moments before concluding my letter. I loved Andrea more than life itself, and I was proud of her, but I also wanted to be frank and honest with her. So with a heart full of hope, I typed these words:

It seems to me that you have been wandering a bit in your life, waiting and wanting to see what your purpose is. I don't know that you will find that in our journey, but I pray that this journey will at

least help you start moving in the right direction
toward that purpose—and I hope you know that
I will always be beside you in that odyssey.

I can't wait to see what this trip has in store
for us!

Love,

Dad

I printed out the letter, put it in an envelope, and went back down-
stairs. I handed it to Andrea and said, "I want you to read this tonight,
before we leave for our trip."

Andrea eyed the envelope skeptically but didn't say anything. She
took it from me and went upstairs. I learned later that she read it, but
nothing about her demeanor indicated that the letter had made any
impression. She didn't say anything about it the following morning,
so I didn't mention it either.

I knew she was excited about the trip, but I hoped that it would
be more than merely a great adventure. I had no earthly idea that the
letter would become almost like a prophecy.

\\\

Before we left for Rwanda, Ebralie told me, "Everyone on a mission
trip can be changed and transformed." And that was my prayer when
we left the U.S. for Africa.

There were no direct flights from Nashville to Kigali, Rwanda's
capital, so our flight path took us from Nashville to Detroit, and then
on to Amsterdam, Nairobi, Bujumbura (the capital of Burundi), and

at last to Kigali—five separate flights covering more than ten thousand miles, with twenty-one hours in the air and thirty-seven hours of total travel. One way.

It was pitch black outside as we made our descent into Bujumbura around midnight. Only when our wheels were about to touch down did the floodlights brighten the runway, revealing that we were indeed at an airport. *How can there be no lights to be seen on takeoff or landing in the nation's capital city?* I wondered. We were clearly no longer in our comfort zone.

After some passengers disembarked and others boarded, we were soon on the last leg of our journey—to Kigali—where we landed, exhausted, at 2:30 a.m. "We've experienced two miracles already," I quipped to Andrea. She looked back at me with a puzzled expression. I explained, "Every flight was on time, and our baggage made the transfers between six separate airports!"

Despite the late hour, a group of about ten people were waiting to greet us. The greeters included Ebralie's sister Mary, along with several members of the Kanombe church where we would visit the next day, and the church's senior minister, Pastor Julius Ngendahayo. Kanombe Presbyterian Church was Mary's home church and had been started by the Mwizerwas home church before the genocide. The people welcomed us warmly and presented each of us with a bouquet of flowers.

We piled into a van to make the short trip from the airport to the *Eglise Presbyterienne au Rwanda* (EPR) guesthouse, located within a complex in Kigali that also housed the Presbyterian church area offices. The EPR guesthouse would be our home away from home. Ebralie had worked with EPR fifteen years earlier, as well as with the Protestant Council of Rwanda, and the people there still held her in high regard. There had been no question whether we would stay in a hotel in the capital city or at the church property: we were friends of Ebralie, and the people in Rwanda treated us as her special guests.

Although it was now around 3:00 a.m. and we had been traveling for more than thirty-seven hours, I was wide awake and my senses were keenly alert. Even at that early morning hour, the city was alive and vibrant. Traffic was thick, and the sound of beeping horns was accompanied by music blaring from restaurants and night clubs along the route. As we lurched toward the church, hundreds of people were out on the streets in brightly colored clothes, walking in every direction on the wide sidewalks that lined our route.

The city was different than those we were used to, and we were in for another rather alarming surprise. Not far from the airport exit, we saw that the police had set up a barricade, blocking all traffic on the main road to and from the airport and pulling over every vehicle. I had read about the roadblocks that were employed during the genocide of 1994, where many Rwandans were either shot or hacked to death with machetes right in front of the barricades.

People back in the States had asked me prior to our trip, "Do you really think it is safe to travel to Rwanda?" Although few Americans truly understood the horrors of what had happened fifteen years earlier in Rwanda, many had seen movies or had heard stories about the genocide. There was a lingering perception that senseless crime was an ongoing issue in the country. Although I had downplayed these concerns when my friends expressed them to me in the U.S., I now found myself nervous as we approached the roadblock.

Our vehicle pulled to a stop, and I could sense some tension in Ebralie. This had to bring back dark memories for her. Here we were, only ten minutes on the ground in Rwanda, and already a roadblock?

We were assured by the calm demeanor of the driver that all was okay. "ID and papers," the policeman said as he came to the driver's window, backed by two other officers with rifles slung over their shoulders.

"Sure," said the driver, as he politely handed over his papers. The policeman slowly looked over the material, coolly glancing over the faces of everyone in the car. He handed the papers back to the driver, wished us a good evening, and waved us through. The locals seemed unfazed by it all, but Ebralie, Andrea, and I all breathed a big sigh of relief.

I later learned that the Kigali police routinely set up checkpoints throughout the city at all hours of the day or night as part of a campaign to control crime. Apparently it was working, as Kigali seemed as safe as any city I had ever visited. Although President Paul Kagame's strict monitoring of the roads, bridges, and other public places seemed heavy-handed to some, others were grateful for the police presence. That feeling must have been shared by the hundreds of people who were out walking the streets everywhere we went.

We arrived at the church guesthouse, and after nearly a day and a half of travel, we happily collapsed into our beds. I later learned that the Presbyterian guesthouse was on the grounds of the offices of the Presbyterian Church in Rwanda (EPR). These were the very grounds where Ebralie had worked for the church before being forced to flee in 1994. Even more, the guesthouse was now managed by William's sister, Zilpa, Ebralie's former co-worker who had originally introduced her to William nearly thirty-five years earlier. It was so special to meet Zilpa and to begin to see the history of the Mwizerwas coming to life before our eyes.

Chapter 16

BUILDING STRONG COMMUNITIES

Early the next morning, Pastor Julius came to visit. For our trip to Rwanda, I packed an extra 150 pounds of gifts—mostly T-shirts from the YMCA that were left over from various membership campaigns and other events. To me, these were the kinds of shirts that usually stay stuffed in the back of a drawer, but when Pastor Julius saw them, he was overjoyed. He particularly liked the saying on the shirts: *Building strong kids, strong families, and strong communities.*

With great passion, and smiling with obvious approval, Pastor Julius repeated the saying several times in English. I smiled as I watched his grateful response. He was especially excited about the children's shirts he found. He said, "I want to give these to our *La Victoire* children's choir—the Victory Choir." We picked out thirty-six shirts of various sizes for the kids, fifteen collared shirts for the men's choir, and another eighty shirts for the regular choir and the church elders. Pastor Julius was very excited about the new "choir robes" his church now owned.

The next day, Andrea, Ebralie, and I arrived at the Kanombe church just before 9:30 a.m. A number of young children ran up to us as soon as we got out of our vehicle. Many of them spoke enough English to ask, "How are you?"—which we heard over and over again. In return, Andrea and I replied, "*Amakuru!*"—the Kinyarwanda word for "How are you?" It was fun to learn a few words and phrases in the children's native language, and the kids got a great kick out of us speaking in their native tongue.

Andrea, Ebralie, and I sat right up front for the worship service that morning in the simple brick church. The congregation sat on thin wooden benches, and people packed together as closely as possible. The kids beamed at us as the choir sang. It was a beautiful sight, with the children singing and smiling, wearing their new T-shirts, and praising God through song. Their voices, accompanied only by a goat-skinned drum, were filled with great enthusiasm and passion for God. The YMCA of Middle Tennessee now had thirty-six little ambassadors wearing its shirts in Rwanda—*Building strong kids, strong families, and strong communities.*

The service continued for a couple hours, and the parishioners almost seemed disappointed when the pastor drew things to a close—a far cry from the tightly scripted services typical of American churches. After the service, we went to Pastor Julius's home for lunch.

I felt so blessed to be able to share time in the home of the pastor and his family, along with some of the church elders. Visiting people in their homes, especially in a foreign country, provides a sense of being immersed there, learning customs and traditions that are impossible to glean from staying at a hotel or eating in a restaurant.

The house was clean but sparse, with only utilitarian furniture in each room. There were no end tables or cupboards covered with knickknacks, and virtually nothing hung on the walls. Pastor Julius and his family clearly saw no need for the material clutter that fills most American homes. Everyone was seated on the sofa or in chairs that were arranged around a small table in the living room. We started with pleasant conversation, and I was glad to learn that the Rwandans at Pastor Julius's home spoke French in addition to their native Kinyarwanda.

French had been the official language of Rwanda, hearkening back to the days of French Belgian colonial ties. While all natives spoke Kinyarwanda, those who attended secondary school (comparable to high school in the U.S.) had learned French. This meant that all professionals and businesspeople of Kigali spoke French, but most of the working poor and rural Rwandans did not.

After joining the Commonwealth community, the president of Rwanda, Paul Kagame, had led a push to have the official language changed from French to English just six months before we arrived. He believed that a quick transition to English would lead to faster economic growth, but at the time of our visit, very few Rwandans yet spoke English. President Kagame's hunch has proven correct, as Rwanda's economic growth in recent years has been exponential.

Growing up in Louisiana, I had studied French in high school, and after a college semester in Paris, I had once been quite fluent. I wasn't quite as fluent now, but between my recollection of decades-old classes and the limited English of our hosts, we soon discovered that we could carry on an enjoyable conversation.

Before the meal was served, a woman brought some soap and a bowl of water into the room and placed it on the table so we could wash our hands. Lunch was served buffet style on the coffee table, with a traditional meal that included stewed meat, rice, fried potatoes, and plantains.

All of the guests, including Ebralie, her sister Mary, and Andrea, ate together with the men, but none of the local women joined us. One of the older women even came in and teased Ebralie and Mary about eating with the men, noting that they were now wearing pants these days rather than the traditional skirts worn by Rwandan women.

Ebralie laughed. "Yes, maybe so," she said, "but when I was a young girl, the men told me that girls could not eat goat meat because we would grow beards like a goat, and if we ate chicken, then we could not have children." Ebralie smiled. "But I proved them wrong. We have five children!"

During our conversation with the pastor and several of the church elders, I commented, "I really enjoyed the passion of the congregation during the service today. I wish the services at my church had such passion."

One of the elders turned to me and said, "You have to understand. You don't need God in America. You already have everything you need. But here in Rwanda, He is all we've got."

While the theology of his statement was totally wrong (we need God in America more than ever), I understood what he meant. Life in Rwanda is hard, and as pleasant, friendly, and joyful as the people are, their lives are difficult. At that time, most Rwandans lived without electricity or running water in their homes. They earned their meager income by tilling their small plots of land, incessantly swing-ing simple handheld plows, carrying water daily from the nearest well that might be miles from their homes, and harvesting fields of sorghum by hauling enormous quantities on their heads—and still had barely enough for a subsistent living. They worked tremendously hard all week long.

But on Sunday? When they gathered together to worship the Lord Jesus Christ, their joy and passion surpassed anything I had ever witnessed. They held on to the promise of salvation and the glory of heaven, and I found myself envious of that.

Chapter 17

AMAZING GRACE

Our visit with Umuhoza was scheduled for later in the week, giving Andrea and me the opportunity to learn more about the experiences of the people of Rwanda, as well as become more familiar with the story of the Mwizerwa family. As we traveled across Kigali on the second day of our journey, I said to Ebralie, "Only fifteen years have passed since the genocide. I can't believe how calm it is here. The people seem so friendly and happy."

Ebralie nodded her head. "I know," she said as she stomped her foot in apparent frustration. "How could that have happened in my Rwanda?" Her sudden rush of emotion clearly showed how raw her feelings were being back in her home country. Undoubtedly, she was conflicted by the fond memories of her past colliding with the feelings of terror that caused her family to flee.

After visiting with friends that day, we were heading back to the guesthouse when Ebralie instructed our driver to take a detour. "We are near my old neighborhood," she explained.

After Ebralie directed our driver through several back alleys, we approached a white brick house with a walled fence and a large metal gate. "This was our house!" she suddenly said with excitement. "This is where we lived!" But her excitement soon turned to a more sullen tone as she pointed to the ditch that separated their home from the road. "This is the ditch where the militia made us lie the day they came to our home, me and all the children, with guns and machetes pointed at us. I don't know how long we laid there—how do you count minutes when you are waiting to die?"

She continued, tears welling in her eyes as she relived the frightful incident, "William was pleading with them." Ebralie paused again, and then spoke softly, yet firmly. "Suddenly there was a gunshot from down the street, and one of the militiamen on the corner fell dead. The others ran toward the direction of the gunshot, then laid in the road and began exchanging fire. We continued to lie there in the ditch, paralyzed with fear. Then William calmly gathered us and led us slowly back into our home, where we huddled on the floor and prayed most of the night. We left the next day. It is terrifying to be back here and relive the horror."

Andrea and I were stunned. Ebralie's story was such a poignant, personal testimony of the pain and peril felt by so many Rwandan families. It was then that I truly realized how privileged we were to have Ebralie as our guide for this journey, as Andrea and I were able to share in these incredible personal encounters.

We later learned that another family had moved into the

Mwizerwas' home after the war. The government eventually established a long and tedious process for displaced Rwandans to claim their lost property. For most people, though, their losses went far deeper.

\\\

A few days later, we had dinner at the home of Ebralie's sister, Mary, and her husband, Jean Marie. Mary and Jean Marie were raising a girl named Grace. I recognized her immediately, as Mary and Grace were part of the welcoming party at the airport the night we arrived.

Grace was celebrating her twenty-first birthday. Her actual birthday had been a few weeks earlier, but she said that she had wanted to wait and celebrate when "Mama Ebralie" would be there. I had thought that Grace was the oldest daughter of Mary and Jean Marie, but that night I would find out about her incredible story.

Grace invited several of her college friends to join us for dinner. The students were friendly and seemed to enjoy the opportunity to meet and talk with Americans. They were curious and asked us many questions, clearly eager to know what we found to be the biggest differences and similarities between Rwanda and the U.S. It was impossible for them to fully understand our two worlds, but it was fun to talk with them.

I was again called upon to use my long-forgotten French—until some of the friends asked if they could practice their English. The students understood the reason for the official language change, but they lamented that they had spent their entire secondary schooling and college years learning French, and now those skills were being thrown out in favor of a different language. They had picked English up quickly, though, and for the rest of the night we switched back and forth between French and English, swapping languages as it suited our topics of conversation.

I couldn't help comparing Grace's birthday party with the many that Darla and I had hosted for Andrea and Alyssa. At our girls' parties, there was always plenty of birthday cake and ice cream, balloons, games, and other activities. At Grace's birthday party, we enjoyed a traditional African meal that included stewed meat with rice, fried plantains, potatoes, and beans.

After everyone had finished eating, Mary brought out a birthday cake for Grace, and everyone sang "Happy Birthday" to her in English. As she blew out her single candle, Andrea and I jumped when her friends and family threw water on her! Apparently this was a local tradition at birthday celebrations, but I couldn't imagine that happening in our home.

Grace then began to speak, and a hush fell over the room. She spoke Kinyarwanda, so I could not understand what she was saying, but I sensed it was important, for her words came with deep emotion. Grace used a napkin to wipe away tears from her eyes several times, and it became clear that she was talking about her past.

I found out later that Grace had been saying how thankful she was to be there, and that she was thankful for her friends and family. "My tears are truly tears of joy for all that God has done for me," she said. She then began talking about Ebralie and how happy she was that she was there to celebrate her birthday with her. The two hugged, and Grace's sister, Jeanette, stood next, thanking God as well. "I was shot six times during the genocide, and at one point I could not walk," Jeanette said passionately, "but now I am able to walk by the grace of God."

I had to choke back my own tears. Hearing these young women tell their stories was overwhelming, even though Grace and Jeanette spoke in a language that I could not understand—but some pain does not need words to be understood.

Finally, Jean Marie, Mary's husband, spoke to the group in English so Andrea and I could understand. "I am so thankful that Grace came into our family. She was the perfect child," he said. "She cared for the younger children as if they were her own siblings. I could not have asked for a better daughter."

With tears now filling all of our eyes, Jean Marie continued. He turned to Andrea and me and said that he was thankful to have us as his guests that night. Then he surprised me by asking if I wanted to say something. I felt really awkward at that point. Being a stranger in their home, I already felt as though I were intruding on a personal and emotional evening. Nevertheless, it would have been rude not to say anything, so I told everyone that even though I did not speak their language, I could feel what was being said. "As a father, I understand love," I said, "and I can feel the love that Jean Marie has for Grace." I turned to Grace and said, "Thank you, Grace, for letting us be a part of your birthday party. I will never forget this."

When I finished talking, I looked at Andrea, and we shared a slight smile. I held her hand as I rejoined her on the sofa. The thankful occasion shared by Grace, Ebralie, and her family that night was the type of moment that had been missing from the Hartley family for too long, but this trip was having the impact that I had prayed for. As I held Andrea's hand, she knew that the words I had spoken to Jean Marie and Grace were also meant for the two of us.

As we headed back to the Presbyterian guesthouse for the night, Ebralie helped us piece together the events of the evening.

She explained that Grace was not the biological daughter of Mary and Jean Marie, but was actually the daughter of Augustine and Esperance. Augustine was one of William's coworkers at the coffee company where he used to work, and Esperance was Ebralie's best friend. In early April 1994, Esperance had gone to a church conference outside of Kigali, and Ebralie was babysitting the then-six-year-old Grace to help Augustine while his wife was away. Ebralie and Grace were very close, and Grace called Ebralie her godmother. The genocide exploded while Esperance was at the conference and Grace was with the Mwizerwas. They would eventually learn that Grace's parents and the rest of her family were slaughtered, with the exception of Grace's sister, Jeanette, whose dramatic story of miraculously surviving six gunshot wounds was told at the party.

Grace had been with the Mwizerwa family in the ditch that late afternoon that Ebralie had described for us, when the militia had pulled them out of their home and threatened their lives. She had also fled with them when they escaped Kigali and traveled with the Mwizerwa family for a period of time as they made their escape. Grace was eventually reunited with her sister, Jeanette, at their grandparents' home.

Ebralie and William raised Grace for a time as part of their own family, but because she was not their biological daughter, the Mwizerwas were not able to bring her with them when they were given visas to the U.S., which broke their hearts. In a sense, Grace had been orphaned twice—once when her parents were killed in the genocide, and again when the Mwizerwa family moved to the United States. With no other option, William and Ebralie requested that Mary and Jean Marie raise Grace and make her a part of their family.

William and Ebralie continued to keep in touch with Grace through correspondence and phone calls, and they paid for her schooling as well.

That evening had turned out to be quite an evening for everyone involved. Attending the party gave me insight into William and Ebralie's family and friends and how the genocide continues to lurk in the background of their lives in so many ways. I was again thankful that I had been able to get an unfiltered glimpse into life in Rwanda and learn so much that a textbook or group tour could not reveal.

I couldn't help but wonder how these encounters were impacting Andrea. How much of this was really sinking in? After just a few days, we had already experienced so much more than I could have ever imagined. I prayed that night, pleading with God to do something big. *Surely, God, this is touching her?* I asked. *Surely this is making a difference?*

Chapter 18

MEETING UMUHOZA

On our last full day in Rwanda, we geared up for what I hoped would be the most memorable part of our journey. The previous segments of the trip had already been very rewarding for us, but now we were getting to the real reason why I had brought Andrea to Rwanda—the afternoon visit with Umuhoza that had been arranged through Compassion International.

Although the reason we had planned the trip in the first place was to visit Umuhoza, I could not help thinking that morning, *Everything else has been so special on this trip. How sad would it be if today did not live up to expectations?* In a strange way, I was actually nervous about this part of the trip.

Compassion had asked us to contact the Kigali office to arrange for our excursion to Murambi, the rural village where Umuhoza lived, so Ebralie made the necessary arrangements for us. The morning of our visit to Murambi, John, a staff member from Compassion, met us at the Presbyterian guesthouse.

The village of Murambi is about seventy miles east of Kigali. It is off the highway that leads to Uganda, but it takes about two hours on a good day to traverse the relatively short distance. There are no major cities along this road, so the vehicle and foot traffic that day were far lighter than they had been elsewhere. Still, there were dozens of people walking on the roughly paved roads. There was no electricity or any running water along the way. The land in this part of eastern Rwanda was much flatter than that around Kigali, and the towns were less populated and the fields less cultivated. After nearly two hours, our SUV pulled off the main road and headed to the village of Murambi.

As we drove slowly through the deeply rutted roads, a dozen or more children who looked to be between five and ten years of age came to see the large SUV slowly making its way along. They spotted Andrea and me and began running behind us excitedly. "Muzungu! Muzungu!" they yelled and laughed. John and Ebralie laughed as well.

"What are they saying that is so funny?" I asked.

Erbalie smiled and said, "They are yelling, 'White people! White people!'"

Andrea and I joined in the laughter and waved at the gathering of children who continued to follow us as best as they could. When we finally reached the Compassion office and shut off the motor, the entourage of children surrounded our truck.

When Andrea and I got out of the vehicle, however, the children pulled back and suddenly became shy, staring at us quizzically. I wondered what they were thinking. We greeted the kids with a hearty, "Amakuru!" They smiled when they heard us speaking Kinyarwanda.

The shyness of the children faded further as they surrounded Andrea, invited by her broad smile. She was in her element as she warmly greeted each child and briefly held their outstretched hands. It was impossible to tell who was enjoying the interaction more—Andrea or the throng of children around her. The scene was not so different than the ones of her with the refugee children at LMV; it was as if she had trained for this moment.

We then walked to the entrance of the Compassion project, with Andrea looking like the Pied Piper as a trail of children followed her. Throughout our meeting, the dozen or more sets of eyes continued to peer through the door and windows, fascinated by these strangers who had come to Murambi.

The staff workers from Compassion ushered us into a small office where we talked briefly about their work here. We were surprised to learn that Compassion had more than 180 projects in Rwanda, each serving about three hundred children. I was awed to learn that Compassion helps about fifty thousand children and their families in Rwanda alone, not to mention the many other families they support around the world.

"We appreciate all of our sponsors," the Compassion representative told us, "but as far as I know, you are the first sponsors ever to visit our project in Murambi."

That news both saddened me and encouraged me. I was sad that the typical Compassion tour did not wander this far into the countryside, though it made sense logistically that they would stay closer to Kigali. I was encouraged, though, that Andrea and I were able to venture off the beaten path. I smiled at the thought that we must be some of the only "muzungu" that some of the village kids had ever seen!

The Compassion project in Murambi operated in conjunction with the Pentecostal church. We learned that Compassion did not normally initiate, build, and operate its own stand-alone ministries in many countries, but instead they partnered with the local churches to serve the children and families in need. Indeed, most of the churches in Rwanda seemed to cooperate wonderfully well. One village might have an Anglican church, while another might have a Presbyterian or Pentecostal church or that of any other denomination—but they all seemed willing to work together as long as the message was about Jesus. They did not seem to be in competition, for they had the common goal of serving the local population. Moreover, they served any of the children in the community whether they attended the church or not. I couldn't help thinking that our churches back home could learn something from these people.

The aid provided by Compassion included school supplies for the kids, as well as food and financial support for the children and their families. For instance, when Compassion supplied a sack of grain because a sponsor in America had supported a child in that family, the entire family benefited from the support, not just the child whose picture was on the Compassion brochure. Everyone we spoke to regarding Compassion's work in Rwanda had nothing but good things to say. That positive report made me feel even better about our family's financial support of three children over the years.

We were talking casually with the Compassion workers in Murambi when a beautiful young lady suddenly pushed her way past the crowd of children at the door and walked into the room. She had a shy smile and big, bright brown eyes. Her dark hair was cut close to her head, which was particularly common in rural Rwanda. Both Andrea and I recognized her immediately. How could we *not* recognize her? She looked just like the photos we had received during the past ten years. It was Umuhoza!

She had recently turned seventeen. She was only a few months older than Andrea, but she was much shorter than what I had imagined. Next to Andrea, Umuhoza appeared younger than she was and more vulnerable. Andrea went to her immediately and gave her a big hug, both girls smiling ear to ear.

After this encounter, Andrea told me, "I was nervous at first, because I just wanted Umuhoza to like me. It was pretty surreal. We obviously had lived very different lives, yet we were connected."

With everything in me, I wanted to hug Umuhoza, as well, but I knew that such a gesture would be culturally inappropriate. I had to practically sit on my hands, but my face was beaming and my heart was full!

Through Ebralie's translation help (Umuhoza did not yet know English), we tried to express to her how thrilled we were to meet her. "I'm so happy to finally meet you," Andrea said, pausing long enough for Ebralie to translate her words into Kinyarwanda.

"Yes," I said, "we have prayed for you every day." I showed Umuhoza her picture that I carried in my wallet to keep her near me and to remind me to pray for her.

Umuhoza seemed a bit overwhelmed by all the attention, and at first she appeared bashful about talking with us. In a soft voice, she told us, through Ebralie, "I am very happy to meet you, as well, and I have prayed for you, too." Though her words were quiet, her smile was bigger than ours, if that was possible.

I just wanted to hug her and tell her how long we had waited for this moment, but instead, we all sat in an awkward but happy silence as the Compassion workers prepared to take us to Umuhoza's home to meet her entire family.

As we got into the SUV for the short drive, the village kids gathered around the vehicle again, staring in awe at Umuhoza, who slid demurely into the back seat, close to the window and next to Andrea. The engine of the SUV revved up, and we eased away from the Compassion center with Umuhoza smiling and waving at the village children seeing us off.

The SUV headed down a maze of dirt roads, past some banana trees and scrub fields, and came to a stop in front of a typical rural Rwandan home. The small rectangular house was made of large mud-bricks, with each brick about the size of a cinder block. The stacked bricks were then spackled with mud, giving the house a smooth finish.

This was Umuhoza's home, but it could have been any of the homes we had seen in the Rwandan countryside. They looked almost identical.

As soon as we arrived, Umuhoza's family poured out of the house to meet us. Of course, Umuhoza was the belle of the ball, exiting from her SUV chariot. With the help of Ebralie and the Compassion workers, we greeted all of the family members, including Umuhoza's mother, Josephine, her aunt, a younger brother, and two sisters. I was especially surprised to see her father, Evariste, emerge last from the home.

Since we first sponsored Umuhoza, we had been told that her father was in prison—but there he was, alive and well and with the family. I assumed there must have been an error in Compassion's data, but I was soon to find out how wrong I was.

Chapter 19

A FATHER
TO THE
FATHERLESS

We exchanged warm greetings all around as we talked briefly
outside Umuhoza's family home. Everyone was dressed in
what looked to be their Sunday-best clothing. I was not sure if that
was out of respect for their American guests or at the suggestion of
the Compassion workers, but the family looked great and Umuhoza
seemed more relaxed now that she was back in her familiar setting.

After a few minutes, Umuhoza's mother and father invited us
inside their home. The door, made from a sheet of corrugated tin,
opened to a large, simple room with a dirt floor. A curtain hung in

the one doorway leading to the back rooms that served as a kitchen and two small bedrooms. Simple wooden chairs were arranged in the main room for the guests. Umuhoza and her father sat on chairs, too, while all the other family members sat on a large reed mat on the dirt floor. We all introduced ourselves—again, with Ebralie's help.

I had brought some gifts, so after Ebralie introduced me, I passed them out to each family member. We had been instructed to keep the gifts simple and modest, which we did. For instance, we brought Umuhoza a sweatshirt with "NASHVILLE" emblazoned across the front, along with a colorful full-length skirt similar to what Andrea was wearing. We also gave her a cross necklace and numerous U.S. coins. Umuhoza's face shone with joy.

I then gave her mother, Josephine, the canvas tote bag that we had used to carry the gifts, and I gave the younger siblings a Frisbee and a soccer ball. As I walked over to present the gifts, I saw a large crowd of curious neighborhood children crowded around the front door, bobbing their heads to get a better glimpse of the strangers, just as the other children had done at the Compassion offices. There must have been at least fifteen wide-eyed children staring and smiling back at me. I wished that I had brought something for all of them, but I hoped that maybe Umuhoza's brother would share the soccer ball and Frisbee.

I saved the final gift for Umuhoza's father, Evariste. I had brought inexpensive windup flashlights to Rwanda, and I gave one to Umuhoza and one to Evariste. As Ebralie explained to him what it was and how it worked, even the Compassion staff members looked on in amazement. They had never seen anything like it before. Evariste held the light in awe. "I can now go out of the house at night," he said, "and the wind will not blow out my candle."

After all the gifts were given, Evariste indicated to Ebralie that he wanted to speak to us. He thanked us for the gifts and said how happy he was to have us in his home. He then thanked us for sponsoring Umuhoza through Compassion.

"My wife and I had tried to have children for several years, but our first two children died during the pregnancies," he said. "We were afraid that we were destined to be childless," he continued somberly, "until Umuhoza was born."

Evariste told us that they were understandably overjoyed at the birth of their daughter. As in biblical families, parents in Rwanda gave their children names that gestured to something remarkable associated with the birth of the baby, or an aspiration or description of something they hoped for in the child's future. "God gave us this baby girl," Evariste said, "so we named her Umuhoza, because that name means 'Redeemer, the Restorer.'"

God had redeemed the hardships of Evariste and Josephine. He had met them in their time of need and blessed them with a child, restoring their wishes, their hopes, and their dreams. I just knew that God must be smiling now, too, knowing that after ten years of our letters, He was finally revealing to us the plan He'd had all along. Andrea and I were here meeting "the Redeemer" ourselves, as God worked and worked to continue the gracious restoration of our own family.

Evariste told us that he had been sent to prison in 1994, when Umuhoza was only two years old, and that he had been released just a month prior to our visit. Although he did not precisely say why he had been imprisoned, it was clear that it was related to the genocide. He was freed in 2009—the year the government leaders of Rwanda initiated the Great Reconciliation. They said, in essence, "It is foolish for us to keep 10 percent of our population in jail. So if you will confess to what you did and ask for forgiveness from the people you have offended, we will let you out of prison based on the time already served." Many, such as Umuhoza's dad, had already served nearly fifteen years in prison. The offer of reconciliation did not pertain to those leaders who had fomented the genocide or to key perpetrators of repugnant crimes against humanity, but instead was intended for many who had committed relatively minor offenses—although in the Rwandan genocide, "minor offense" is a relative term.

Each town set up councils, known as *gacacas*, to hear the confessions and pleas for forgiveness. Ordinary members of the communities, including survivors of the genocide and family members of those slain, listened as tens of thousands of former participants confessed to their killings, asked forgiveness, and submitted themselves to the judgment of their neighbors. The offended parties were not required to extend forgiveness, but in most cases the community decided that the inmates had been punished enough, and the local people decided to forgive the repentant perpetrators. These community trials were held in public and happened all around Rwanda. This public communal act of forgiveness was likely the most significant factor in the nation's ability to break the bondage of the past and move forward into a better future.

Umuhoza's father thanked Andrea and me especially. He said that when we supported Umuhoza through Compassion International, we had actually helped his entire family to have food and a place to live. He said, "When I went to prison, I didn't know how my family was going to survive, so I prayed and asked God, 'How can I provide for my family?'"

Evariste looked at me. "He sent me you. Your generosity came to us at the time of our greatest need. The money you gave bought beans and corn and helped to keep my family fed. Thank you." He then said something that I could not have imagined. "I want to thank you for being a father to my family when I couldn't be, when I was unable to be here."

My emotions had been running at near fever pitch since arriving in Rwanda, but when Evariste thanked me for being a father to his daughter, I nearly lost it. Tears welled up in my eyes, as well as in his, and we both embraced in a strong hug, followed by a tight handshake.

I was sitting in Evariste's hut thinking, *Here I am as a father full of regrets. How could a good, faithful dad have allowed what happened to my daughter to happen? Yet this man is thanking me for being a father to his family. Who knew—while my family was falling apart, I was helping to keep his family together!*

It stirred me deeply and made me think. I hadn't been able to explain why I felt compelled to bring Andrea to Rwanda, and up to this point, I still had no idea why I was there, other than God had told me to go. But in that moment, I knew why I was there. Yes, it was for Andrea—but it was also for me.

Umuhoza's dad then went to the back of the house and returned with a gift for me. It was a picture of his family that Compassion had taken shortly after Evariste had returned home from prison a few weeks earlier. It was obviously a priceless treasure to him, and I accepted his kind gesture reluctantly. As I gazed at the photo, I realized that each of the family members had on the same clothes in the picture that they were wearing for our visit. The clothes were clearly their Sunday-best clothes worn for special occasions, such as the day your dad gets home from prison—or the day we had come to visit. The kindness of his gesture melted me again.

Emotionally drained, I was glad when somebody suggested that we go outside so the children could play with their new gifts. Soccer is a favorite pastime for Rwandan children, but real soccer balls are difficult to acquire. A couple of kids standing outside the door had a homemade soccer ball. They had started it with a balloon, then collected plastic scraps and wrapped them around the balloon over and over until it was roughly the size of a soccer ball. When they got the ball the right size, they wove string around the mass of balloon and plastic. The finished product worked surprisingly well, bouncing and rolling along much like the real thing. Still, the real soccer ball was a big hit, and the kids began playing with it right away.

Apparently, the kids had never before seen a Frisbee. At first, they weren't quite sure what to do with it, so Andrea and I showed them how to toss it like a plate. The kids lined up behind Umuhoza to take turns throwing it. Their excited giggles, smiles, and expressions of delight at such a simple gift were more reminders of how blessed we are in America.

I smiled, too, as I thought, *What a wonderful, weird picture this is! Here I am, a middle-aged "muzungu" from Tennessee playing Frisbee with the village children in Murambi, Rwanda, on a beautiful Wednesday afternoon in July.* I tried as best I could to soak it all in. I noticed that Andrea was having a similar response, with her emotions bouncing back and forth between tears and elation.

"My pain definitely connected me to the people I met in Rwanda," she said later. "When you share pain with someone, you really feel that empathy; there's a power in that."

As we played with the children and shared time with Umuhoza and her family, I was struck by the redemptive nature of the situation. Ebralie and her family had fled Rwanda in total fear as the incessant killings were everywhere. Yet here was Ebralie leading me back to

Rwanda, to the home of a man who had been jailed because of the genocide, to meet his daughter and family whom I had been supporting for a decade. All three families had been broken, yet through this incredible connection, we had all experienced healing. Only God could weave our lives together in such an unlikely, unbelievable, beautiful tapestry. I am so grateful to Him for it!

All too soon, it was time for us to leave. The visit had flown by. We had been at Umuhoza's home for more than an hour, but I really didn't want to leave. We gathered together for one final picture, gave each other our last hugs, and waved goodbye. As we piled into our SUV for the return trip to Kigali, I wondered if we would ever see these new friends again.

I was thankful that our time with Umuhoza and her family had been so special. This culmination of a yearslong journey had exceeded all of my expectations. Government programs, humanitarian non-governmental organizations, and even Christian relief agencies can show pictures, videos, and statistics, and they are helpful—but Umuhoza and her family put such human faces to the process. Nothing can compare with experiencing the real thing—seeing the poverty and subsistence-level living, and also seeing what even a few dollars can do to help. For thirty or so dollars a month, less money than Darla and I would spend on a casual dinner out, I had been able to be a positive influence on Umuhoza's entire family. And for that small amount of money, time, and effort, her father considered me a surrogate father to this precious child—a child whom God used to change all of our lives. I was so blessed to be a part of it. I had truly received so much more from the visit to Rwanda than I could have ever given to Umuhoza and her family.

The ride back from Murambi to Kigali was a time for reflection. I couldn't help but think back to the circumstances that had brought me to Rwanda and had allowed me to be in the little village of Murambi on July 15, 2009. The wheels had really been put in motion almost ten years prior to the trip, at the Amy Grant Christmas concert, when Amy Grant asked the audience to find the Compassion International brochure that had been placed beneath each seat, inviting us all to sponsor a child. Similar to the parable of the seeds in Luke chapter 8, those brochures had been scattered like seeds in a field. As in the parable, some seeds settled in weeds or fell on rock and withered away, but at least one seed fell on fertile soil, sprang up, and was bountiful. That bounty is a beautiful Christian Rwandan young lady named Umuhoza, the Redeemer and the Restorer—and Andrea and I got to be part of her life.

Chapter 20

FILLING IN THE BLANKS

The morning after our visit to see Umuhoza, Ebralie, Andrea, and I left Kigali together on a flight to Nairobi. Ebralie was leaving us at that point to meet the mission group from First Presbyterian Church. We said our goodbyes with heartfelt expressions of thankfulness. It was hard to believe that I had barely known Ebralie before this trip; the moments we had spent together in Rwanda were the kind that forge close, lifelong friendships. "We'll see you back in Nashville," we called out to one another as we waved goodbye. "And we'll exchange pictures!"

In Nairobi, we had ten hours to kill as we awaited our night flight from the international airport back to Nashville. Knowing we had this long layover, Ebralie had arranged for David, a family friend, to meet us at the airport and show us around Nairobi.

David was a fun, energetic man in his mid-twenties who had been born and raised in Rwanda. His grandfather had been an elder in the Anglican Church, and his father was an Anglican priest. David's grandfather, along with many other church leaders, had been killed in the genocide.

Despite the sadness regarding the past, David was an upbeat, eclectic combination of academic, entrepreneurial, and philanthropic interests. He had earned his master's degree from Syracuse University and made a good living coordinating tourist trips to Kenya and other African safari sights. With his academic background and his family's story of surviving the genocide, David had also become an accomplished speaker at conferences arranged by the UN and others. Encouraged by the more altruistic leadership of the Rwandan president, Paul Kagame, David was an optimistic and passionate person who wanted to make a difference in the new Africa.

As he showed us around Nairobi, my head was swimming, trying to absorb all of his new insights and the things we had already seen and done while in Africa. After a great day of sightseeing and shopping at the street market, aided by David's expert negotiating skills, we headed to a restaurant for a meal before the long flight home.

We talked effortlessly with David, telling him the things we had seen and done. We bombarded him with questions, trying to fill in the blanks of the mosaic of Rwanda that we were trying to piece together.

Throughout the trip, Andrea had been quietly absorbing everything around her. I had wondered how much she had really processed in regard to all the things that we had seen and done, but she began to open up at the restaurant with David, peppering him with questions. "What are your thoughts regarding Western charity?" she asked. "Do the aid and gifts really make a difference?"

"I understand why the West might have donor apathy for Africa," David said. "After all, the West has given billions and billions of dollars in aid to the continent, and sadly, most countries have relatively little to show for it." David lamented that Africa had some of the poorest people of the world yet seemed to have some of the world's richest political leaders. The injustice of corruption would certainly test the resolve of any charity trying to help the continent.

Having said this, David was optimistic that Africa was nearing a tipping point in turning the economic tide. "In recent years, thousands of native Africans have obtained needed education from the West and are now returning to Africa for the sole purpose of giving back to their homelands."

Andrea pressed on. "What is the best way to help the people of Rwanda, or the people of Africa as a whole?"

"Great question," David replied. "When it comes to helping Africa, charity is not a sustainable model; only capitalism is a sustainable model. If the model is based on charity, the benefit stops when the giving stops. On the other hand, if the benefit is based on a viable economic model, that benefit can be perpetual."

\\\

"I'm really happy that we had that time with him," Andrea told me when we were at the airport. "David really helped me understand what people in Rwanda are facing."

An old proverb claims, "Everyone who visits Africa will fall in love with it and will want to return." As we settled in for our flight home, I could understand that sentiment. As I thought of the people we had met and the experiences and inspiration we had enjoyed, I hoped that someday we could return with our entire family. For now, I was hopeful that the trip had impacted Andrea the way it had impacted me.

I thought back to the letter I wrote her the night before we left—how I had hoped she would have time to reflect upon her life, her goals, her dreams, and even her purpose. I had prayed that the Brentwood Bubble would burst, that she would see God at work and learn more about His work in and through us. I had suggested to her that we had a chance to see God mold us into better people.

When I wrote those words, I was hopeful but uncertain of their full potential. I never could have imagined how true they would turn out to be!

Chapter 21

HEALING THROUGH SERVING

When Andrea returned from Rwanda, she was a changed person. No, she didn't become a perfect angel overnight. She was still our independent, feisty teenage daughter. But after the trip to Africa, Darla and I did not have a single serious behavioral issue with her— no incidents with drugs or alcohol or flagrant rebellion ever again.

Andrea had found a sense of purpose in helping others, and it made all the difference in her own life. Her grades improved dramatically; in fact, she got straight As her senior year. She spent much of her spare time continuing to work with Legacy Mission Village. Before our trip, Andrea had served at LMV a couple of times a week.

During her senior year, after our return home, she went to LVM four days a week almost every week of the entire school year.

She cut ties with the negative influences, including some of the darker friendships she had formed during her junior year. At that age, seniors in high school always want the acceptance of their peers, but Andrea willingly turned her back on that pressure. She even gave up cheerleading, an activity she loved and had done since sixth grade, so she could spend more time helping with the refugee children at Legacy Mission Village.

Some of her friends would ask, "Where do you go after school every day?"

Andrea always smiled and said, "Come along and see." Even though friends sometimes accompanied her to LMV, none of them caught the passion that Andrea had. Although her friends' indifference disappointed her, it did not deter her from serving. She continued to show up, even when it meant going on her own.

It was an astonishing transformation, and everyone noticed. As Darla observed Andrea's newfound sense of purpose, she said to me one evening, "It seems that Andrea has found her place and purpose. Things are looking up—for her and for us."

Regarding Andrea's takeaway from Rwanda, William Mwizerwa wisely observed, "She was wounded, but she saw other people who were more seriously wounded than her and still having hope. By working, touching, coming in contact with people who had been seriously wounded, she realized, 'My pain can be healed.'"

Andrea herself would say, "It wasn't until I visited Rwanda that I made a definite decision that I was going to move on. It totally changed my life. It saved me. The whole time, my family was fighting for me. They really wanted me to find peace. If it wasn't for my family ... my family motivated me to start living again, and to forgive and move forward."

Thanks to the improvement in her grades at school, Andrea had a wide variety of options when it came time to choose where she wanted to attend college. It warmed the heart of this Louisiana boy when my daughter chose to enroll at Louisiana State University. Because of her newfound passion for Africa and its people, she majored in International Studies with a concentration in Africa.

My joy regarding our trip was tempered only by the fact that our whole family had not been able to share in what we had just experienced. Andrea and I, along with Ebralie, effusively attempted to convey our enthusiasm to the rest of the family and friends, but our words fell short of what we felt in our hearts. I knew that one day I would see to it that the entire Hartley family would make the trip to Rwanda.

Two years later, that opportunity came. Legacy Mission Village hosted another trip to Africa, and this time William was going along. This would be his first trip back to Rwanda since fleeing his homeland and all of his family's earthly possessions during the genocide of 1994. William was now a U.S. citizen, and with the comfort of his U.S. passport (and the passing of another couple of years), he finally felt fully confident in returning to his beloved Rwanda.

Not only were William and Ebralie going, but they were also taking their youngest children, Tim and David, back to their homeland—and the whole Hartley family was tagging along too. It was certain to be an emotionally moving and profoundly spiritual time. It would be a different sort of trip than Andrea and I had experienced since this would be a working mission trip in which we would join other volunteers. It was not only an opportunity to experience a different culture, but it was a genuine chance to serve, and I was excited for my whole family to experience it together.

As it turned out, Andrea was already in Africa that summer. As a student at LSU majoring in International Studies with Swahili as her foreign language, Andrea had gone to Africa to complete her language studies at Dar es Salaam University in Tanzania. She had some time in between when her class ended and our trip, so she looked to find a mission opportunity while she waited for us to arrive overseas. Through Ebralie, Andrea was connected to African Christian Tours and Safaris (ACTS) in Kenya. Andrea could volunteer with them for two weeks and then join us when we arrived.

Andrea was most interested in the ACTS program for providing volunteers to work at Angel's Orphanage outside of Nairobi, where a staff of just two loving ladies were given the task of caring for about twenty orphaned infants. Working with the orphaned children touched Andrea's heart so profoundly that she immediately began to ruminate on ways to get her college friends to join her in serving in Africa. Our family met up with her in Nairobi at the end of her time with ACTS, and we all traveled together to Rwanda for the LMV mission trip.

After we landed in Kigali, we went through immigration and secured our bags. I immediately noticed a major difference from our previous trip. Everyone was speaking English. It was incredible that in the two short years since we'd left, it seemed that the entire country had become fluent in our language.

We were once again greeted by members of the local church, who drove us to the familiar Presbyterian guesthouse. Our families were joined by about a dozen other people from the U.S. Since each family had made individual arrangements for travel, it was at the guesthouse that we caught up with the other members of the mission team, including the Mwizerwa family.

When I saw William, I asked enthusiastically, "How does it feel to be back?"

His response was more reserved than I had expected. "It is good," he said, but his smile was slow, almost timid. I could tell that this trip would come with a variety of mixed emotions for him.

William later said, "It was amazing to me. I enjoyed seeing how the country had changed. But it was painful. It was like taking the cover off." That was William's way of saying it was like pulling the bandage off an old wound.

On that first afternoon in Kigali, William left the guesthouse to walk around downtown Kigali. He was curious as to how much the city had changed and who he might see. When we reconnected with him for dinner that night, I asked him what he thought.

"It has changed so much," he said. "I was disappointed to find that I did not see anyone that I knew."

"It's been seventeen years, William," I reassured him. "It would be hard to expect to see anyone you know." I would soon learn not to doubt William's faith.

The Kanombe church that Andrea and I had attended two years earlier had built a new, larger sanctuary, helped greatly by donations from the First Presbyterian Church in Nashville. It was perfect harmony, with the Mwizerwas' new church in Nashville helping their former church in Kigali expand. The main focus of this trip was helping to put the final touches on the new sanctuary. We would be doing chores like painting, cleaning, and assembling new pews.

The first morning, as our mission crew traveled by bus across Kigali to the Kanombe church, William suddenly became quite animated as he called to his sons. "Tim, David—look! Those are the walls of the coffee compound. That is where I worked!"

We all peered out of the bus windows to see the large coffee compound on the hillside above the road. The compound was outlined by an imposing white cinderblock fence, capped by coils of razor wire. William continued speaking, seemingly to no one in particular. "I always regretted that we did not live on the coffee compound. I was the only senior employee who did not live on site, but circumstances were never right for us to move there." As his tone turned more somber, he said, "But as it turned out, the fact that we did not live there saved our lives."

Ebralie continued the story. "We had been sheltered in our home as the genocide broke out," she explained, "but we talked by phone to our friends Augustine and Esperance, who lived at the coffee compound. They assured us that if we could make it to the compound, we would be safe there. And," she reminded us, "we were babysitting their daughter Grace and felt the need to get her back to them." At that point, Ebralie's voice became more emotional, much like the tone I had heard two years before as we were outside of their former home.

"So William loaded us all into a car," she continued, "and we tried to make our way to the compound. But just before we arrived there, we came across a roadblock. It was terrible, with militiamen everywhere and dead bodies strewn all around. The militiamen dragged us out of the car and had us lie in the street with machetes to our heads. William was negotiating and doing everything he could, but the situation was very bad."

Then Ebralie's pace began to quicken. "Suddenly, there was a great explosion, with dust flying everywhere. I don't know where the bomb came from—I think it was sent by God. But in the midst of the dust and confusion, William was somehow able to get us all back in the car, and he flew backward down the road—and we were eventually able to make it back to our home."

Ebralie took a deep breath before continuing. "What we did not know at the time was that the roadblock saved our lives. We learned that on that very day there was a massacre of all those who lived on the coffee compound. The militia had stolen some buses and drove them to the compound. The men in the buses convinced the guards that the troubles were over. They then invited everyone to get onto a bus, claiming that they would be driven to a safe place for food and drinks. Slowly and nervously, the men, women, and children who lived at the compound came out and boarded the buses."

As we sat mesmerized listening to the story, Ebralie again became more solemn. "It was a trick. Once everyone had boarded the buses, they were driven out to the city dump, where they were taken off the buses and mowed down with machine gun fire. The only two survivors were the daughters of Augustine and Esperance, who were partially shielded by the bodies of their parents. Both girls were wounded, and they waited until nightfall before making their way to their grandparents' home. Unfortunately, the oldest daughter died from her wounds, but Jeanette survived, despite being shot six times. It is only because of Jeanette that we learned what had happened at the coffee compound."

I was stunned by the story—not just because of Ebralie's emotional account of the events, but because Andrea and I had met Jeanette on our trip two years earlier. She was Grace's sister, whom we had met at Grace's birthday party. Jeanette had been praising God at the party, saying she had been shot six times and could not walk but had since been healed. I was now stunned to hear her whole story. Despite the horrendous tragedy that she and her family had been through, she was able to praise God, saying she was the luckiest girl in the world.

Before this trip, I was afraid that our visit to Rwanda could not live up to the power and emotion of the journey that Andrea and I had taken two years earlier. This story of the roadblock, the coffee compound, and Jeanette quickly showed that this trip, too, would have plenty to teach us—and we were just getting started.

Chapter 22

UNFORGETTABLE FORGIVENESS & RECONCILIATION

After a couple of days of work at the Kanombe church, we had a rest day scheduled so we could return to Remera, William's home village. William was anxious to visit his boyhood village and see his cousin Philibert, who still lived there.

It was great to see William enjoying time with the cousin he had not seen in so long. William was no longer anxious. He now seemed totally relaxed, ready to enjoy time with friends and family. After seventeen years, he was back home.

After lunch, the Mwizerwa family was going to visit the gravesite where William's mother, sister, two aunts, and a nephew were buried. While they were living in Nairobi, William and Ebralie would learn bits of information from back in Rwanda. Sadly, most of the news was of the death of relatives and friends. From these reports, William knew that these family members had been killed in the genocide, but he did not know the circumstances.

We loaded into the caravan of cars that we had taken on the trip to Remera and then snaked our way down some dirt roads until we came to a stop where William's mother had lived. William and his family made their way down the hillside to the graves, but the rest of the group stayed back at the cars to allow the Mwizerwas some privacy.

After the family returned to the cars, the Hartley family ended up in the car driven by William, and ours was the last in the line of cars. As we followed the others around a bend, hardly a mile from the burial site, William slammed on the brakes. "That's Margaret my mother's best friend!" he exclaimed. We all looked at the same time to see an older Rwandan woman emerge from a modest mudbrick hut.

William put the car in park, got out of the vehicle, and slowly approached Margaret as he called to her in Kinyarwanda. Margaret looked at him cautiously at first and then suddenly threw her arms up and gave William a warm hug. It had been seventeen years since William had been in Remera, and it was surely a wonderful surprise for the two of them to accidentally find each other this way.

We watched from the car while the two of them talked. The conversation appeared to turn more serious. We were too far away to hear what was said, and the whole conversation was in Kinyarwanda. But when William returned to the car after about ten minutes, his face was pensive and his mind seemed a million miles away. It was a quiet drive back to the Presbyterian guesthouse.

After dinner each night, our mission team held a Bible study and had time for reflection, which I have always found so meaningful and uplifting on mission trips. That night, after Scripture was read and our group engaged in a lively discussion about what we had seen and done on the trip thus far, William began to speak. Always reserved and quiet, he seemed especially uneasy.

"After we visited the graves of my mother and family today," he began quietly, "I ran into my mom's best friend. She told me that my aunt was involved in the death of my mother and other family members." The deep emotion in William's voice filled the room as he continued. "Aunt Esther had been an orphaned Hutu as a little girl, as a drought had hit Rwanda in 1949. My grandfather was a Christian man, and he adopted the little girl and raised her as his own. She grew up as a sister to my mom. I remember her well, as she helped raise me as a little boy." William's voice quivered as he continued. "She is one of the few people that I can remember as a little boy who is still alive. I remember when she cared for me, when she fed me."

William looked up slightly. "I have been praying about this since I returned from Remera today, asking God for guidance as to what I should do. I have decided that I am going to go visit my aunt tomorrow. I want to learn what she can tell me about my mother's death. I have called Philibert to let her know that we are coming, and that we come in peace. I don't want her to be nervous or scared."

The missions group sat in utter silence as William softly said, "Please pray for me and my family, as I know it will be a difficult day."

I couldn't imagine what the next day would hold for William and his family, but we all prayed fervently for them that night.

The next day, while the rest of us returned to Kanombe church to continue our help on the new sanctuary, William and Ebralie, along with Tim and David, returned to Remera. It was difficult not to think about William and the family throughout the day as we continued to paint, clean, and prepare the new sanctuary. We returned to the guesthouse by early evening, where we ate and again assembled for Bible study.

As I was about to enter the room, I spotted Ebralie, who had just gotten back from their trip to Remera. She looked emotionally drained.

"How was your day?" I asked.

"It was really, really difficult," she said. "It was good for William, but it was a tough day. Lots of tears were shed." I gave her a hug and told her that we had all been praying for them.

Our group had already started our Bible study that night when the remainder of the Mwizerwa family entered the room. They sat quietly as the rest of us continued discussing the evening's Bible lesson. When our conversation ended, William began to speak. "Ebralie and I prayed all night last night about visiting my aunt Esther," William said. "I was nervous because I did not want it to become a dispute. In Rwanda, it is illegal to confront someone about the genocide, as there are rules to avoid revenge and to maintain the unity and reconciliation. My plan was not to confront her, but rather to repair the relationship. Everyone in my mom's family had been killed by the genocide. Even though the devil may have used my aunt, she is the only person left on my mom's side of the family.

"When we arrived at her house, Esther was in her front yard, and she hugged us warmly and praised God for being able to see us again. We handed her our gifts to show that we came in peace, and she welcomed us into her house. Because Philibert had called to let her know we were coming, her home was already full with her daughter, two daughters-in-law, and seven grandchildren.

"We first talked about old times and family memories," William said, "and then I asked her if she could tell me about what happened to my mom and my aunts."

William gathered his emotions and continued, slowly and methodically. "I could see that this question made her family anxious, as they feared her answer could cause trouble. But Esther began to tell us what happened. She said that my mother and aunts had been sheltering in my mom's home in Remera, trying to hide and wait out the killings. After a few days, the home was attacked by militiamen, and the family fled to Esther's house for help, thinking they would be safe. But when they got there, they were attacked and killed by Esther's sons, my cousins."

As William finished, the whole room was silent—except for the sounds of soft sobbing and the wiping of tears. But William wasn't done. "The room was full of tears as she finished, and the family was nervous about my reaction. I wanted them all to know that they were all safe, and that I wanted peace. So I picked up a pitcher of water nearby and laid the basin that we had brought as a gift on the floor, and I washed her feet."

An audible gasp was heard in the room. "I washed her feet," he continued, "because I wanted her to know that she was forgiven. She needed to be forgiven. All of Rwanda needs to be forgiven if we are to move forward. And I forgave her not just for herself but for me as well. No one needs to carry the guilt of sin with them, and no one needs to carry the sin of hatred."

William told us that his aunt was stunned by his gesture and thanked him over and over for his forgiveness. She told William that she had been overwhelmed by guilt for all those years, and she thanked God that William had the strength and courage to forgive her.

After many tears and hugs, they were able to share their stories of the last many years. The aunt's sons had disappeared following the genocide, and she had not seen or heard from them for the past seventeen years. William shared his family's story since their escape, and he introduced his sons, Tim and David, to their great aunt.

As our Bible study group caught its breath, we slowly surrounded William and the family, laid our hands on them, and prayed for them.

"You don't know how unforgiveness has a hold on you," Ebralie later observed, "until you meet the person who has wronged you. I was happy to see her grandson and the wives of her sons. We cried, we hugged each other, and we promised the peace of God to each other."

Looking back on that day, William said, "People think you forgive to help the one you are forgiving. I forgave, and it helped *me* to heal. It was what I needed, what I believe the whole country needed—forgiveness. We can't repair what happened in the past, but what we need is to show love and show the gospel and to repair the country. Forgiveness is liberating."

I was deeply affected by William's self-effacing, forgiving spirit. I wondered what I would have done. I would have a lot of ideas about what I would do when I visited someone who had done as horrific a thing as Esther's sons had done. I would *not* have thought of taking a bowl of water to wash her feet. I have heard a lot of Bible stories. I have heard a lot of sermons and testimonies. I will never hear one any more powerful than the one that night at our Bible study.

The Hartley family had to leave Rwanda a day earlier than others, so as we prepared to depart, I asked William what he thought about his first trip back. He was more relaxed than he had been the first time I asked him the question, and he talked about how healing the trip had been for him. He said that while it was difficult learning about the fate of his mother and aunts, he did find some peace in at least now knowing what had happened.

William went on to say that he was still hoping to learn something about his father's fate. He knew that his father had been home when the trouble started, and he knew that his father never made it back to Remera. But other than that, he had no idea what befell his father. "I am still hopeful that I can learn something about what happened and how he died."

A week after we returned to Nashville, Darla and I went out to dinner with William and Ebralie, and I asked William if he had heard anything about his father's fate. He said that the night after our family left, he was approached by a man who could tell him what happened.

William learned that his father was with a group of people who were trying to escape from their village. As they moved from place to place, they stopped in the papyrus reeds to hide, as they knew that the militia was everywhere. At that point, they decided it would be better to divide into smaller groups to avoid detection. The group said a prayer, and then went in two different directions.

Soon after they split, one group heard screams coming from the other group, which included William's father. Unfortunately, his group was discovered by the militia, and were killed.

I put my hand on William's shoulder and told him how sorry I was for him to have to learn this. William paused and then said, "No, it is good. I am glad to finally know what happened. And it warms my heart to know that my father prayed just before his death, and that he was with other Christians when he died. I can now have peace."

So on William's last night of his first return trip to Rwanda, he was able to close that dark chapter in his family's story. The final pieces of the story had been told. I was glad that William had finally learned what had happened to his family, and I was thankful that he was such a strong man of God that he could find peace in that knowledge.

The fate of William's father struck me as a parable for all of Rwanda—and for all of us as well. Whether William's father lived or died had depended on the seeming randomness of the path he had taken. While our choices may be much different than those faced by William's dad, we are nonetheless impacted by the decisions we make every day. But like William's dad, if we keep Jesus with us everywhere we go, we can ultimately find peace, no matter what comes our way. We never know what lies around the corner, but with Jesus in our lives, we can know our eternal destiny.

Chapter 23

BEAUTY OUT OF BROKENNESS

The trip that Andrea and I had taken in 2009 had been so transformational for both of us that although I prayed that our 2011 family trip would be powerful, I was skeptical that it could match that first experience. I had prayed fervently that the rest of the family could share in the redemptive nature of our journey, and my prayers were certainly answered. Each of us was very deeply affected by what we had witnessed—the opportunities to serve, the sights we saw, and the stories we heard. William's example of forgiveness and reconciliation was an especially healing experience for us all, and none of us was quite the same after we returned home.

After our trip, Darla and I became even more engaged in serving at Legacy Mission Village, and all of our children developed a deeper connection to mission work and to Christ. Serving at LMV as a family helped us to continue to feel connected to missions, even though we were now back home in the U.S.

Andrea witnessed William's willingness to forgive those people who had hurt him so severely, and although the pain that she had carried was much different than William's and Ebralie's, she saw the power of forgiveness to heal hearts and to give people the ability to move forward in their lives. She realized that you can never forget the pain you have experienced, but you can allow God to redeem it and use your brokenness for good in your life and in the lives of others.

The following year, Andrea returned to ACTS with six of her LSU sorority sisters, and this time her older sister Alyssa joined her. Like Andrea, she had been moved by her various encounters in Rwanda, and she wanted to continue to give back to the people and the continent that had meant so much to her. Their task on this mission was to serve at a school for the deaf in Kambui, north of Nairobi. Many of the children had been abandoned, as superstitious Kenyans thought that their deafness was a sign that these children had been cursed.

The classes were divided by age, and the young American women were given in advance different subjects and concepts that the school hoped they could help teach while they were there. The college students took their tasks seriously and worked hard to develop posters, projects, and crafts to help communicate the message of their subjects. They were delighted to find that the students loved the bright colors and textures that they were able to bring to the classrooms. The teachers were amazed at how much the girls were able to teach, and how much the children learned, in only two weeks.

"The classrooms were just gray and drab when we got there," Alyssa said. "It was so great to see that as we posted the projects on the walls each day, the classrooms slowly changed into bright splashes of color. Bit by bit, the walls became covered with all kinds of shapes and colors. Just like the children themselves, the classrooms became transformed."

The Americans had gone through an orientation before volunteering in the classrooms, and they had been told a bit about the students in each room where they would serve. Alyssa was told that her class included a boy named Vincent who was much more developmentally disabled than the other children in the class. When Alyssa first met the teacher and the class, the teacher pointed out the boy. She said his name was Benson, not Vincent, and she encouraged Alyssa not to let Benson slow down the class.

As Alyssa and her volunteer partner began to teach the class, they found that the boy the teacher called Benson, while slower than the others, could indeed do the projects they assigned. So Alyssa worked one on one with Benson while the other volunteer led the class.

The room full of students seemed to really come alive as they were taught their lessons using colorful construction paper, scissors, glitter, and glue. When that day's work was finished, Alyssa and her assistant helped the children write their names on their projects and hang them on the walls. Alyssa worked with Benson to sign his name on his project so that it could join the others. She helped him spell out *Benson*, but he was very slow and unsure as he wrote.

It bothered Alyssa that she was told in orientation that the boy's name was Vincent, while the teacher said his name was Benson. So she talked to the volunteer coordinator about the issue, and the coordinator said she would check the file in the head office to confirm the correct name.

When Alyssa arrived at the school the next day, the coordinator gave Alyssa the answer to her question. The boy's actual name was *Steven*. Steven! This poor boy, deaf and deemed too slow to learn, had been at the school for nine months, and he had been called by the wrong name that entire time!

When the class did their project that day, drawing and writing the name of their favorite animal, Alyssa again helped the boy with his project. When it was finished, she then helped him write his name on the artwork. As she started to help him spell *Steven*, the boy's face lit up and he quickly finished writing his name—and his hippo proudly got hung on the wall.

Sometimes when you go abroad on a mission trip, you really find yourself. And sometimes you find a Steven—a person who is lost in the shuffle or overlooked in his world. Alyssa brought lifelong memories home and left behind a proud little boy. She will never forget Steven; and with his name hung proudly on the wall with his hippo, I pray his class and his teacher will never forget him either.

Nate was deeply affected by the trip to Rwanda as well, though true to his nature, he expressed his elation in a more reserved manner. Back in school during the fall of 2011, his AP English teacher gave the class an assignment to write an essay about an abstract concept. Nate chose to write about beauty, but he did not describe it in terms of vacuous movie stars or pop music artists. He began his essay like this:

> The summer of 2011, my family and I traveled to
> Kigali, Rwanda, where we stayed at a Presbyterian
> church guesthouse. While there, we volunteered

to paint a church, and we spent hours sharing in
the antics of the local children. One day we visited
an orphanage. We took all the kids on a bus to a
clearing where we gave them toys and games and
let them have a free day, playing all day with us. In
this moment, looking at all of the children running around with ecstatic expressions overtaking
their faces, I said to myself, "This is true *beauty*."

Our quiet child, Nate, didn't say much about how he felt, so reading
this essay helped me realize how profoundly moving he had found
our experience in Africa; our journey had impacted him exactly as I
had hoped it would.

Of course, there was another girl, about Andrea's age, whose place
in our family remained important well after our first trip in 2009.
Umuhoza and our family continued to correspond regularly. In fact,
after that first meeting, our letters became even more personal. We
visited Umuhoza again in 2011 while on our mission trip, and this
time we were able to bring the whole family to meet her, with William
as our translator. It was wonderful to see that she and her family were
doing so well. Evariste again expressed thanks for the assistance of
Compassion and the help it provided his family. He was also pleased
that the aid helped with school supplies, and he told us that all of
their children were doing well in their studies.

Shortly thereafter, Umuhoza graduated out of the Compassion
project, just as Subbu from India had done years earlier. But this time,
William had gotten to know the pastor from Umuhoza's church,
and he was able to continue communicating with her. We learned
that Umuhoza wanted to go on to college—the first person in her

family to pursue higher education—and we knew we wanted to help.
The Hartley family was thrilled to sponsor a college scholarship for
Umuhoza through Legacy Mission Village, and even more thrilled
that our connection to this wonderful young woman and her family
lived on.

\\\

Back at LSU, Andrea was so often talking about Rwanda and Kenya
and mission work that her friends nicknamed her "Africa." Her
enthusiasm had drawn six young women to Kenya the year before,
and they all loved the experience. The ripple effect started from there:
now it wasn't just Andrea who couldn't stop talking about her mission work but also Andrea's six friends. Interest began to grow, and
now they were organizing a much larger trip. Andrea planned to
lead twenty-five girls from her sorority to work at an orphanage in
Zimbabwe, again organized through ACTS. The women worked all
school year raising funds, mainly by working at the concession stands
at LSU home baseball games. They had coined the phrase "Sisters
in Service" the year before when their small group had served at the
school for the deaf. Sisters in Service was back in action once again,
but with a lot more sisters this time!

As we prepared for this trip, I helped to keep up with the money
and accounting for all twenty-five girls. Just a week before the trip,
I noticed that one of the young women had failed to make her last
payment. I asked Andrea, "Is Nicole still going?"

"I don't know if she's going to make the trip or not," Andrea said.
"I think there are some things going on with her, but I'm not sure."

I contacted Nicole's father. "Randy," he said, "I don't think Nicole can do it. She's not had a good year, things aren't going well with her, and I'm not sure I want to reward her with a trip to Africa."

I paused, ready to say "okay," but something made me offer my perspective. "I certainly understand that," I said. "I'm a dad who had a daughter go through quite a bit. She was in some deep stuff. When I took her to Rwanda, that trip changed her life and her perspective. Now she's the one who is leading this trip." I pressed forward with one final thought. "Maybe this trip is an opportunity and not a reward."

"Yeah, I hear what you are saying," he said. "But I don't think so."

"Okay. I'll refund what I can," I offered, "but unfortunately the plane ticket at this late date is nonrefundable." The dad said he understood.

A few days later, he called me back. "Randy, is it still possible for Nicole to go on the trip? What you said stuck with me. I've been talking with some friends and counselors, and they said you might be right. Maybe this is an opportunity."

The trip for Nicole was back on, and she accompanied Andrea and the other sorority members on the trip. They blogged each night about what they had experienced that day, and we followed along back in the U.S.

Reading their comments each night with Darla was fun and very moving, but I was anxious to see if Nicole would post anything that would clue us in as to how her trip was going. On the fourth night, it was her turn to post. "Before I came on this trip," she wrote, "I didn't even know why I was coming. I didn't know what this would be like." Nicole alluded to the fact that she had been going through some difficulties in her personal life. "But when we got here, we were working in an orphanage, and I met my favorite little girl. She is a quiet, sweet, beautiful little girl. Her name is Ashley. Then today I learned from the teachers that Ashley is HIV positive and both of her parents have died of AIDS. When I heard that, I had to leave the classroom. I'm not very religious, but I went outside in tears, fell on my knees, and prayed for the first time in a long, long time."

Nicole continued. "Ashley had told me that her dream one day is to go to college, and I am praying that somehow God will allow her dream to come true."

As I read Nicole's heartfelt words, knowing that there had been some question about whether Nicole would even go on the trip, my eyes filled with tears. I was so moved. Though I didn't know what was going on in Nicole's life, I knew something was broken. I couldn't help but think of our struggles with Andrea a few years before, and I prayed that Nicole would be touched and transformed in the same kind of way that Andrea had been.

After reading Nicole's blog post, I immediately sent an email to her dad. "I don't know if you've seen Nicole's blog tonight—I hope that you have read it—but it has moved me so deeply. I'm in tears."

Nicole's dad replied quickly. "Far better than the blog was the telephone conversation I had with my daughter tonight. I'm so thankful that you talked me into allowing her to go on this trip."

With so much of what we do in life, we never get to see the outcome of our efforts. We often don't get to see the long-term impact of the good that we may have done. The same is true of ministry and mission work. As I said before, it is like sowing seeds, both for those served and those who serve. We are never sure which seeds will grow. We do not know which seeds fall on rocks and which ones fall on fertile soil. I don't know what happened to Nicole or Ashley. I wonder about the deaf student, Steven, at Kambui, and the infants at Angel's Orphanage. Did those seeds grow?

I don't know, but I do know one thing. I know that one seed grew. I know that Umuhoza has grown into a loving and caring adult, and I know that Andrea was a seed that came back to life! I can't change the whole world on my own, but I know that I have changed at least a few people, including myself—and that makes all of it worthwhile.

Chapter 24

KINGDOM BUILDING

Two years after our 2011 family trip, we returned to Rwanda for another mission trip sponsored by Legacy Mission Village. Again we traveled with all of our children. William, Ebralie, their daughter Aimee, and their younger sons also went on the trip along with many in the youth group of Covenant Presbyterian Church in Nashville, as well as some of their parents. Our primary mission work on this trip was to help build new homes in an area just outside Kigali, as well as to host a vacation Bible school (VBS) at the Presbyterian church in Remera that William attended as a little boy.

We were again lodging at the EPR guesthouse. The EPR compound was also the site of the Presbyterian church offices, where Ebralie had worked with William's sister, Zilpa, before the genocide.

It was at this compound that Zilpa first introduced William to Ebralie. Many of the former offices had been turned into guest rooms. The one where William and Ebralie were staying was actually Ebralie's former office!

This trip also happened to coincide with William and Ebralie's wedding anniversary. They did not know that Zilpa and the hosts in Kigali had planned to throw them a surprise anniversary party. Zilpa and the other hosts had contacted as many old friends as they could find and invited them to surprise the two at the guesthouse. Many of the guests were from the Mwizerwas' former church, and most of them had served in the choir with William and Ebralie. Among those attending was the friend who had hosted the Mwizerwa family in Kenya when they were refugees so many years earlier and Ebralie's high school teacher, Michel, who had become a close friend of the Mwizerwa family.

It was a joyous, moving evening, with these old friends laughing and crying and sharing so many memories. Before the meal, William said a beautiful and heartfelt prayer, thanking God for letting all of these friends survive and now get together, and also remembering the far greater number of friends who had not survived the genocide. The evening ended with the old choir members singing the Kinyarwanda hymns that they had sung years ago in their church. Every song was sung from memory—special memories that I'm sure for many had been buried deep below the more painful ones that had followed. But for that evening, it was nothing but fun, fellowship, and faith.

One of the members of the mission team remarked to Ebralie how close all of these friends seemed, especially given how long it had been since they had seen each other. Ebralie said, "We have lost so many people from our past, so we cling especially tight to the ones that we still have."

The next morning, the mission team headed to Remera for the first day of vacation Bible school. As part of the leadership team for this trip, Darla was in charge of coordinating supplies for VBS. Ebralie had been in communication with the local church in Remera and had told our team to expect eighty children for the week. Wanting to be overprepared, Darla decided that, just to be safe, she and her team would assemble enough coloring books, crayons, crafts, and activities for 120 students.

When we made it to the Remera church, we were suddenly overwhelmed. Rather than 80 or even 120 participants, our bus was surrounded by the cheers and screams of more than 250 children. I looked at Darla and I could tell she was panicked. She loves to have all the details planned, but those well-laid preparations for this particular VBS were already out the window. "This is going to be joyous chaos!" she told me on the bus. "Time for Plan B, whatever that is!"

Darla and the other volunteers quickly set about the task of adjusting to the size of the program. They took the coloring books that they had and tore them into thirds. Crayon boxes were divided up, and pencils were broken in two and resharpened so that every child got one. I was reminded of the story of Jesus with the two fish and the five small loaves. Regardless of how many people we thought we would have, the supplies were divided in such a way that no one went without!

Aimee led the VBS at the church because she spoke Kinyarwanda. When she asked the local church administrator about all the extra children, he said, "Yes, our church expected about eighty children, but when everyone heard that people from America were coming to host VBS this year, children from all over Remera showed up!" He was apologetic, but we didn't mind. We loved every moment of the "joyous chaos" of hosting so many children.

One of the crafts for the younger children was to build a picture frame out of popsicle sticks, and on the frame they wrote, "I am a child of God." The leaders took a picture of each child, printed it on a color printer that we had brought, and put the child's picture in the frame. We were surprised by how much they loved their pictures, but Aimee explained that these children and their families rarely, if ever, got a photograph of themselves, so getting one was extra special.

Aimee then told us an exchange she had heard between a child and her mother when the mother came to walk her daughter home one day. The little girl had finished her picture frame, and it was complete with a beautiful picture of her smiling from ear to ear. When the mother arrived, the girl ran up to her and could not wait to show her the craft she had made. When she handed the picture and frame to her mom, she asked, "Is that me in the picture?"

"Yes, that is you," the mom replied.

The girl took the frame back, looked at the picture, and said, "I'm beautiful!" She was beautiful. After all, as the writing on the picture frame said, she was a child of God!

While we were in Remera for VBS, many of the teens and men had the opportunity to help build new houses for people whom the church had identified as most in need. These were the same type of mudbrick huts that we had visited Umuhoza in four years earlier. The mud was mixed with straw right on the spot, packed tightly in a wooden mold, and laid out along the ground to dry.

They were then stacked to form the walls of the home, with fresh mud used as mortar between each brick. Each brick was about the size of a cinderblock. Local craftsmen were hired to actually lay the bricks, but the volunteers were used to transfer them first. It was quite a sight to see it all come together and to know that we had a small part in helping to build a family a home.

Each night during the mission trip, we met for Bible study, just like we had done two years before. One night, a teenager from Nashville complained that he did not think we were building the homes fast enough. "We could be getting so much more done," he said. "But when we arrive, we spend so much time talking. And the lunch breaks are so long, we seem to be spending so much time goofing off. And we could work later, too. It just seems that if we worked longer and harder, we could do more."

As he finished, many in the mission group nodded in agreement with his assessment. William then spoke, and as usual, it was time to listen. William acknowledged the teen's observations. "You are right," William said. "If we worked harder and visited less, we could build the houses faster. But think about the real purpose of our visit. I have to tell you, the people of Remera really don't need us here to hand them bricks and mud. They know how to build homes."

William paused, waiting for his point to be understood before continuing. "We did not come here to build homes. We came here to share our faith and our fellowship. When we are spending time with the local people before we start working, and during those long lunches, that is what you are doing."

William smiled. "Life is hard for the people of Remera. They have to work hard for everything they have—their food, their water, what little money they have. But you being here gives them hope. It shows them that people care. They need that hope, and that is what you bring from America."

For the next few days, the pace of our work slowed. We spent more time talking and laughing with the locals before we started, and lunches stretched a little longer. We even stopped early one day and had an impromptu soccer game with the local villagers in a bumpy cow pasture. The pace of building the mud huts had slowed, but the pace of building God's kingdom had greatly increased!

Our final day in Remera was a Sunday, so we planned to have church with the community that we had served for the week. On this particular Sunday, the Remera church was packed. Just as with VBS, when word got out that our group from America would be there, everyone in the area came to church. The wooden benches of the church were filled to capacity, and many more people stood in the back.

Similar to most churches, the Rwandan church received an offering. Plates were passed, just as they are in churches the world over. What struck me during this offering, though, was that at the same time as the offering, people came forward and placed items such as eggs, oranges, and bags of coffee beans on the altar. After the ushers brought the offering plates forward, the pastor picked up the eggs and held them high, and people began to raise their hands and shout.

We were confused as to what was going on, but Ebralie explained that these were offerings made by those without money, and the pastor was now auctioning off the items to those in the congregation. The winning bidder would come forward, put their bid amount in the offering plates, and leave with the items.

When we reached the last item, a bag of coffee beans, those of us on the mission trip began to bid, quickly raising the price to outbid each other. While other items had gone for two hundred or three hundred Rwandan francs, we quickly bid the bag of coffee to ten thousand francs. The auction stopped, and the winning bidder from our team went forward to place the money in the plate and collect his coffee. The entire church erupted in applause. Those ten thousand francs equaled about twenty U.S. dollars, but for one member of our team, it surely was the best bag of coffee ever purchased!

After the church service, the congregation gathered behind the church for a special ceremony. The previous year, Legacy Mission Village had conducted a special Christmas promotion asking people to "buy a kid" for fifty dollars. Each donation allowed us to purchase a baby goat to be given away to those identified by the church as those most in need. The success of the program allowed us to give away fifty goats to various families in the church.

As we gathered together, I noticed that many of our goats were pregnant. I mentioned this to Ebralie, who said, "To buy this many goats in a village at one time would be difficult. We would drive up the price of goats! So we have been buying goats for months and building our herd so that we can give them all away now. During that time, some of our goats have gotten pregnant."

"Well, we must have purchased some promiscuous goats!" I quipped.

"Oh, no," Ebralie said. "That is a good thing! Baby goats are valuable."

"Then some of these people are going to be lucky and get two goats."

Ebralie smiled. "No, there is a wonderful tradition in Rwanda. If you are given a goat, then you must in turn give away the first-born baby to a neighbor in need. It is your duty to pay the kindness forward."

What a beautiful concept! Here we were, giving a goat away to those identified by the church as those most in need, and even then, when these people were blessed with a baby goat, they would bless a neighbor with a similar gift. I loved that tradition!

Chapter 25

FROM THE SEEDS WE SOW

In 2011, when we had last been in Remera, William had learned about his Aunt Esther and her involvement in the death of his mother and sister. After forgiving her family and washing her feet, William and Esther promised to stay in touch. Technology had advanced, so cell phones had become relatively inexpensive and quite popular in Rwanda, and William had been able to call her from time to time.

Now that he was back in Remera, he wanted to visit her. After the goat-gifting ceremony, the Mwizerwa family went to visit Aunt Esther while the rest of us returned to the guesthouse for our last evening in Kigali before returning home.

At that evening's Bible study, William told us about the visit with his aunt. He said that after they had visited for a while, his aunt's daughter asked, "Do you remember what I promised you last time we met?"

"No, I'm sorry," William said. "I don't remember."

"I promised you that I would start going to church again," she reminded him. "I had stopped going to church. But after you washed my mom's feet and forgave her, I have been to church every Sunday since."

William went on. "My aunt then told me that her daughter had married a Muslim man and turned away from her Christian faith. After I left, the daughter asked her, 'What would give a man the strength to do such a thing?' My aunt told her, 'Come back to church with me and find out.' So the daughter started attending church with my aunt, and then she converted back to Christianity."

William beamed, thankful for the ways God had worked in him, and hopeful of the ways He would continue to move. "So if you want to know why we forgive," he said, ending his story, "it is because it saves souls. And what greater calling do we have as Christians than that?"

\\\

On our previous mission trip, our main project had been to help the Kanombe church prepare its new and much larger sanctuary for service. Pastor Julius told us that shortly after the church moved into the new building, a mother with a disabled child approached him and asked if she could use the old sanctuary to meet with some mothers who had children of their own with disabilities.

Pastor Julius was soon surprised to learn how many of the women in the Kanombe neighborhood fit this description; a number of the children had severe cerebral palsy, and others struggled with other sorts of special needs. Most of these moms had kept their children hidden at home because of the social stigmas and prejudices, with people assuming the kids were cursed. But Pastor Julius welcomed them. Within a month, there were thirty or forty mothers bringing their disabled children to meet regularly at the old sanctuary.

To the church, the building was just the old, unused sanctuary, but to these ladies, the building was a *true* sanctuary—a welcoming safe haven where they could spend time with others who understood their situation without judgment.

When we returned to Rwanda in 2013, our mission group visited the women, and we were amazed to see so many mothers with disabled children in the former sanctuary. I was never prouder of our teenagers than on that visit. They sat right in with the mothers and their children, holding the children, singing to them, and interacting as best they could. It was a simple act of kindness, but these Rwandan mothers were so happy. Their children, who had been rejected by their society, were being readily accepted by our group. It filled the mothers with far more joy than I could have ever imagined.

That impromptu visit became the genesis of another project sponsored by Legacy Mission Village. We were all so moved by these mothers and their children that the board of LMV began working with the Kanombe church to start the first school in Rwanda for developmentally disabled children and their families. LMV raised the funds to build the school, pay the teachers and a therapist, and provide supplies to help support the school.

The parents believed that their children would be quite limited in what they would be able to learn. But within a short period of time after opening the new school, and with the help of some amazing college-aged volunteers provided by LMV, virtually all of the children had shown that they could learn and speak and even start doing tasks such as feeding themselves. It was an amazing transformation, not just of the children, but of their entire families.

For the Rwandan mothers, the fact that Americans would come to Kigali and spend months as unpaid volunteers was hard to comprehend. Even more amazing to them was that these Americans would spend their time every day working with these children whom others had told them were worthless and hopeless! The moms said, "If these volunteers are willing to come and help our children, our children must be valuable." How ironic that only a few years earlier, it was the bright-eyed excitement of refugee African children that had caused Andrea to feel and know her value.

One of my favorite parts of a mission trip is to take a group of American teens to Rwanda and to watch the transformation that happens in their lives. Prior to the trip, the things that they view as important often create a warped sense of self and self-worth. Frankly, the same is often true of their parents, siblings, teachers—and most of us in America. We live in the land of plenty, and it is easy to lose sight of what is really important.

However, when the kids go to Rwanda, they are astonished to meet people who have so little of our material trappings and yet seem so happy. As William often reminds the volunteers regarding impoverished people in Africa, "Their lives are tough, but they look at this life as temporary. God has something better for us in heaven." This eternal mindset is why church services in Rwanda are so spirited—and we need to bring that spirit back to our home churches in the U.S.

\\\

We visited Umuhoza again in 2013 and also in 2014. She was in college by then, so we took a taxi and visited her at her college north of Kigali. She could speak a bit of English at that point, which was a good thing, because for the first time we didn't have William or Ebralie with us to translate.

We learned on that visit that her father had been ill. We also learned that her home, the mudbrick hut that we had first visited five years earlier, was having structural problems. I promised Umuhoza that we would help her family build a new home. I talked with William and Ebralie, and they worked with her family to make arrangements to build the new home. Umuhoza's father was ill, so Umuhoza became the general contractor for the new family home, and Ebralie sang her praises: "She is very smart and very tough. She would not let any of the workers know that a *muzungu* was helping to pay for the house. She knew that if they found out, the price would double!"

The house was finished the following summer. Ebralie and Andrea made their way out to Murambi for an official ribbon-cutting ceremony to dedicate the new home. The trip was particularly special for Andrea because Umuhoza was now fluent in English, so they were able to have their first complete conversation without translators.

Umuhoza has since graduated from college, and she recently married. We were deeply moved that she invited us to attend her wedding. "Outside of my family," she said, "there would be no more special guests I could think of than the Hartley family."

Unfortunately, we were not able to attend Umuhoza's wedding because of COVID-19 travel restrictions in 2020. We sent her a heartfelt letter of congratulations and a gift expressing our regret, and she replied with the kindest note that reflected the special relationship that we had built with her. "I am very happy to have good (surrogate) parents like you," Umuhoza wrote, "who cared for me from when I was a young girl. Because you have taken me as your own daughter is the reason why I wished to have you here on my wedding day. I know that you love me and pray for me. I had prepared a place for you as my father at the ceremonies because I have two fathers! God bless you for all you have done for me, in all of my life. I love you so much! Your daughter, Umuhoza."

When I read Umuhoza's letter, I was overwhelmed with gratitude. It is I who have been blessed by this special daughter who has meant so much to our family.

Chapter 26

BRINGING
OUR STORIES
TO LIGHT

Beyond the obvious blessings of our trips to Africa, I felt privileged to learn so much more about the Mwizerwas' history each time we traveled together. Pieces of the story were revealed to me like parables, at just the right time and at just the right place: being at Grace's twenty-first birthday party with Ebralie; passing by the coffee company with William; the "chance meeting" with the friend of William's mother near her gravesite—and all of the stories told by William at the Bible studies.

Ebralie loved to say that God wastes no pain, that God loves to take your pain and turn it into your passion. He had surely done that with the Mwizerwa family, and He had surely done that with Andrea. He had even done it with me. *Perhaps*, I mused, *others could find hope in their hopelessness by sharing our brokenness.*

The more I thought about it, the more it struck me just how unusual it was that we would receive a brochure at a concert that would lead to us sponsoring Umuhoza, a little girl from Rwanda. Then, what are the odds that William and Ebralie would flee the 1994 genocide in Rwanda and land almost in my backyard in Tennessee? And at our family's lowest point, who could have guessed that Andrea would receive a letter from Umuhoza that would be influential in helping get our daughter back on the right track? It was almost as though Somebody else was directing this story. All I had to do was write it down.

So I did. My scribbles eventually formed the foundation for a documentary film, *Through the Valley*. Before we released it, my own extended family members were unaware of the trauma that our nuclear family had been through. I am quite close to my family, but I had hidden our hardships with Andrea from them. In anticipation of the film, I called them all and let them know about the struggles we had been through. In many ways, my previous reluctance to share these difficult facts with them mirrored Andrea's fight to hide her troubles from Darla and me, but sharing them, as I was continually reminded, brought healing, encouragement, and hope.

The documentary was a critical success, winning three awards, including being chosen as the 2014 Religion Documentary of the Year by the Religious Newswriters Association. This positive reception led me to help write and produce *Beautifully Broken*, a movie based on the documentary, which was released in 2018. We hosted a movie premier of *Beautifully Broken* in Franklin, Tennessee, at a theater in

The Factory, a complex of offices and shops that was once a Jamison Bedding factory. On the night of the premier, as William Mwizerwa walked the red carpet as one of the VIP guests, he reminded me that his first paying job in the U.S. was sewing mattresses for Jamison. From sewing mattresses at Jamison to hosting a movie premier at their old factory—that twist of fate seemed to symbolize everything about the Mwizerwa journey.

The movie serves as a tribute to all that God has done for three divinely connected families. God forgives, and God restores. He takes what is broken and turns it into something *beautifully broken*, something that He can use to help others and bring Him glory. That is what He has done for our family, and now, I hope, that is what our film is doing for others.

Putting our family's deeply personal story on screen was not without its moments of trepidation, especially for Andrea. She frequently said, "I don't want to be known as *that girl*. The story has shaped my life, but I don't want to live there in the past. I've moved on."

Consequently, we debated about how much of Andrea's experience we wanted to include in the movie, and I gave her the option. "You tell us," I said, "and if there's anything you don't want us to include, we won't do it."

Andrea ultimately seemed at peace with the story being revealed. "Dad, if you're going to tell the story," she said bravely, "you have to tell the whole story."

While I appreciated her honest and forthright attitude about it, I knew that it was going to be a wrenching experience to have some of our family issues played out on the big screen for everyone to see, but the feedback we have received from those who have seen *Beautifully Broken* has justified our decision. Many people have told

Andrea and me how the film has affected them positively and how proud they are of her for telling her story.

They especially appreciated that Andrea was willing to bring her molestation experience into the light. The response from one young lady at a college particularly stands out. After showing the movie, I saw a young woman loitering at the back of the crowd, waiting for the line to thin out. Having hosted dozens of screenings, I had learned to see the signs of the people who were really touched by the film—people who wanted to talk. After nearly everyone else had left, this young lady about Andrea's age came up to me and said, "I struggle with depression. Some days are worse than others, and today was a really bad day."

She began to cry as I held her hand in mine. "I don't know why I even wandered in here tonight," she continued, "but I'm glad I did. That film is the best thing that has happened to me in a long time. I need to go home and call my father."

I asked if I could give her a hug, and she nodded yes. I gave her a warm fatherly embrace, much like the embraces I had given Andrea so many times over the years. I didn't get the young woman's name, but I thanked her that night for her courage and for passing along those comments to me. Whether she knew it or not, she and others like her are a great blessing to my family and a reminder of God's continuing grace.

Even for our family, memories of the past remain painful. But at least now, the past is in perspective, and it has led us to a place where we can all move forward. I have said many times that I would not wish the hand we were dealt on anyone, but I praise God that I have a Lord and Savior who can make any cards a winning hand. I don't think for a second that my God wanted Andrea to go through what she went through or that He wanted the Mwizerwas to endure what they did. However, I believe that what Andrea went through led her to where she is today and that she is doing what she was called to do. I believe that the Mwizerwa family would say the same thing about their own difficult experiences, for they have since been used by God to serve thousands of refugees throughout Tennessee through Legacy Mission Village.

Evil exists in the world, and no one is immune to it. Being a Christian does not mean that evil won't find you, but being a Christian does mean that you have a God who will help you carry that pain. Just as I could not prevent the pain endured by Andrea, my heavenly Father does not protect me from all pain. But as a father, I was there to help Andrea through her pain, and our heavenly Father is there to help us through ours. There were times when I questioned where God was in our story, but even during the times I could not see Him at work, He was still there—causing all things to work for our good and for His glory.

\\\

Mark McFerran met the Mwizerwa family when they first arrived in Nashville, when they enrolled at Brentwood Academy where he was part of the administrative staff. Mark later moved on to work for Lipscomb University in Nashville, where he helped lead the "I am Second" program, a multimedia movement that produces short videos, billboards, and other messages by individuals willing to tell their stories, acknowledging that "Jesus Christ is first, and I am second."

Mark had seen our documentary and was moved by Andrea's story. He asked me if Andrea would be willing to do an interview for

"I am Second" and tell a brief portion of her story. After thinking it over, Andrea agreed. While confident at first, Andrea became an emotional wreck the night before she was to tell her story. Darla tried to calm her down, but she was inconsolable. "I can't do it," Andrea said over and over. It seemed as if she were wallowing in a soupy mixture of anger, sadness, and embarrassment.

"Andrea," I told her, "if you don't want to do the interview, you don't have to do it."

"But I've already promised," she said.

"Mark will understand," I assured her. "I'll just explain that it is difficult for you to handle the emotions. If you want me to talk to him, I'll be glad to do that. You don't have to do the interview if you don't want to."

Darla later reinforced what I had said, but she also reminded Andrea that her story could be helpful to a lot of young girls. "You have an important message," Darla said, "that other kids might want to hear."

I called Mark to give him a heads-up and to let him know that Andrea was experiencing a real emotional tug-of-war over the interview. I let him know that he should be prepared to adjust if necessary. Mark was gracious. "No worries," he said, and he was right. We didn't need to have worried.

The next morning, Andrea got up and went with Darla to the interview. She was nervous since it was her first time to speak about the documentary or its details in front of a live audience, but once the interviewer invited her to tell her story, she plunged in and shared her heart. She sat in front of the audience, so genuine and composed.

"I'm going to try not to cry," she said with a smile before continuing. "I grew up in Brentwood with an acute sense of the meaninglessness of all the materialism that surrounded me. I struggled with it, but that was the only life I knew. My parents said, 'You are searching for your purpose,' and I was—but I was having a hard time finding it.

"Once I got to high school, I was trying to find meaning in unhealthy ways. . . . A few incidents sort of characterized that downfall. When I was twelve years old, I was at Crockett Park for the Fourth of July to see the fireworks. We were around a group of older guys who were drinking." Andrea paused and sighed heavily. "It's never easy to talk about," she said, struggling to maintain her composure.

She took a breath and continued. "But I was molested, and I did nothing about it—and the guilt that I had for letting it happen stayed with me for a really long time, for years, until I talked about it again."

Andrea shrugged slightly and said, "That's why I'm talking about it today. It is so important to voice those taboos. I remember that night, I thought, *Well, Andrea, you've decided; you're a bad kid.* I sought out that destiny from then on.

"My freshman year of high school, I definitely got more into the drinking, partying, and drugs. I had a boyfriend who was older than me. We had both gone through similar traumas, so we became dependent on each other, but it wasn't in a healthy way. It was a very codependent relationship, and it got pretty emotionally abusive, sometimes physically abusive, so that also broke my spirit.

"Even after that [relationship] ended, I continued to self-medicate, and I would go on stints with whatever drug I could get my hands on. I would run away and…" Andrea choked up for a moment. "And I put my parents through hell. I remember thinking, *God, wherever You are, You're not there for me.* A few times I laid in bed going, *I don't want to wake up tomorrow.*" Andrea paused again and struggled to contain her tears.

"Meanwhile, my parents were doing everything in the book; I'm so lucky to have parents who care so much. They were doing everything to save me and fix me. I went to therapy, which was good, because it did get me talking about things that I had buried for years. It is amazing to me now how long I kept some really emotional secrets and just let them kind of fester inside me.

"I also went to rehab, which really helped reintroduce my connection to God and made me realize that God hadn't forsaken me. Really, I had been pushing God out of my life, I think, because I didn't want to deal with the pain.

"One moment of divine intervention that set me on the right path and gave me a purpose was when we met the Mwizerwa family. They were refugees from Rwanda who had escaped the 1994 genocide. Their son became good friends with Nate, my younger brother, and we got to know each other's families.

"The Mwizerwas started a nonprofit organization in Nashville called Legacy Mission Village that helps other refugees come in, acclimate, learn English, and find a job. They asked if I wanted to volunteer in the children's department, tutoring, teaching basic English and math to children anywhere from five year olds to thirteen year olds.

"Volunteering really built my own self-esteem. There were two kids in the class who really touched me—Phineas and John. They were six years old at the time, and they were like my little 'buds'—and my little minions, too! They were so cute, and they totally looked up to me. So how could I be worthless if these kids say, 'We love you, Miss Andrea. We miss you!' That's when I started to feel, *Okay, maybe I do have a purpose.*"

Andrea went on to describe the trips to Rwanda, especially the trip on which William had met with his aunt and had washed her feet. His actions had made a profound impact upon Andrea. "Wow, I thought I knew betrayal," she said, with an expression of amazement at William's self-effacing actions toward the woman who had helped facilitate the slaughter of his family members.

"Even more profound than how quickly evil can manifest," Andrea observed, "is how forgiveness can heal, and that is what we witnessed. This wasn't just a war between two groups; this was families turning against family members."

However, Andrea explained, the effect of forgiveness in Rwanda was stronger than the trauma that had come before it. "The power of that is so huge," she said. "It has basically healed the country. It seemed that everyone I met in Rwanda during that trip embodied the story of Jesus and His willingness to forgive us."

Andrea then offered a keen insight into her attraction to Africa. "I think the reason I am obsessed with East Africa is because those countries have gone through a lot of adversity but have come out triumphant. For me, I decided that I want that to be *my* story—to go through adversity and to be triumphant, and to forgive. My experience in Rwanda taught me the importance of forgiving—forgiving others and forgiving yourself. That was totally life-changing."

Andrea then told about leading several groups of her college friends to Africa and about her work with ACTS. "As much as I give," she said, "I feel like I am never able to give as much as I receive, which is a frustrating cycle," she added with a laugh. "But the Bible teaches us not to seek our own well-being but the well-being of others, and I think God abundantly rewards you for that.

"Another reason I keep going back," she continued, "is that I have never seen such undistracted faith, just pure faith. The people cling to the promise of salvation." Andrea concluded her testimony by saying, "I know that God's love is redeeming because I've seen it in the groups that I've brought over to Africa, the volunteers, and the people I have met in Africa. And He also saved my life." She took one more deep breath and smiled. "My name is Andrea Hartley, and I am second to my Savior."

I was working when Andrea was scheduled to give her testimony, so I couldn't be there, but Mark McFerran called me afterward. I was afraid he was going to say that she hadn't shown up or that she had not been able to go on stage. Instead he simply said, "Your daughter—wow, what a testimony!"

When I saw a video of Andrea's interview, I could not contain my own tears. The story shined a spotlight on sexual abuse and also opened the door for helping African refugees. It was as though God was taking us full circle—from pain to forgiveness to helping others to healing.

Chapter 27

LOOKING THROUGH STAINED-GLASS WINDOWS

About a year after my first trip to Rwanda, I saw Amy Grant at a luncheon event in Nashville. I knew I had to approach her. "You don't know me, and you aren't aware of this, but you changed my life."

"I did?" Amy responded with a smile. No doubt, Amy had heard many similar statements from others, so she may have thought I was referring to one of her songs or albums.

"One of your concerts changed my entire family forever," I explained. I shared with Amy about finding Umuhoza's Compassion

International material under the seat at her concert.

"You planted that seed under my chair, and God used it in ways you can't even imagine. We not only sponsored three children— we went to Rwanda to meet one of them." I told her briefly about Andrea's transformation.

"That is so lovely to hear," Amy said. "My daughter and I just returned from Rwanda where we were visiting a child we sponsored there, too."

We talked further about our experiences with Compassion and how we received so much more than we ever gave. It was great just to be able to thank Amy for being willing to lend her name and talent to Compassion's work with children. So often when seeds are scattered, the person who spreads them doesn't know whether any took hold or not. I wanted Amy to know that the seed she planted took root in our lives.

Beautiful how it all turned out.

As Andrea was nearing her graduation from LSU, she was determined that she wanted a career that would allow her to work in Africa. But uncovering those opportunities was tough, and Andrea became discouraged. She called home from LSU shortly before graduating, crying. She simply said, "I feel Africa slipping away."

As dads do, I helped talk her through this crisis. I reminded her that she had been on three different mission trips with ACTS. Not only that, I reasoned, but she had actually coordinated the last trip for twenty-five college students. She also spoke Swahili and had graduated with honors with a degree in International Studies. "Just contact the people you worked with for your mission trips," I said. "Surely they will find you to be an attractive candidate." She did, and she has been working in Africa ever since.

Andrea still has a feistiness about her. It was that quality about her that allowed her, at not quite twenty-one years of age, to hop on a plane and move to Africa to work full-time with ACTS. She was the first American ever to be hired by ACTS as a full-time group leader.

The offices for ACTS are at Brackenhurst, a well-known retreat and conference center north of Nairobi. Andrea's lodging was in a basic cinderblock cabin on the back edge of the compound. When she first arrived, there were spiders crawling everywhere. Andrea did find bug spray in the cabin—a local brand called "Doom." Andrea wrote in her journal that night, "How am I going to survive Africa if I used an entire can of Doom my first night?!?" But survive Africa she has. She has now lived in Kenya for more than six years.

It was tough for her at first. She was alone. The other people she worked with lived off the compound and already had their family and friends—but Andrea persevered and eventually thrived.

Andrea was a group coordinator for ACTS, so she laid out itineraries for people like her—people yearning to serve God in Africa—and helped facilitate their time on the continent. Because she lived on the compound, she was on call 24/7, even weekends and nights. If anyone needed anything done after normal work hours, they called Andrea. Her entire social life revolved around the groups that were coming to do volunteer work in Nairobi and other areas of Africa.

Eventually, much to our chagrin due to safety concerns, Andrea convinced us that she needed to get her own apartment so she could have more free time, which she did. She moved to an area where many like-minded members of the expatriate community live, including workers from Christian groups and international aid agencies, so she discovered a great sense of camaraderie there.

Andrea acclimated to Africa so well that she seemed almost like a native. On one occasion, she found a special friend who confirmed that truth to her. While leading a tour at the Kitengela Glass Factory on the edge of the Nairobi National Park, Andrea decided to sit outside at a roadside picnic table across from the factory and enjoy the quiet as she waited for her tour group. No sooner had she sat down than a Sykes monkey came out of the forest, hopped onto the picnic table, and sat down right next to her. "Hi, buddy," Andrea smiled. "How are you doing?"

The monkey looked into Andrea's eyes, crawled over closer to her, then reached for her hand before placing it on his back. Andrea didn't flinch but began talking to her wild friend as she slowly scratched its back the way you might do to a pet cat or dog. Whenever she would stop petting and scratching the animal, the monkey would reach around and put her hand on its back again.

When the tour group came out, they were surprised to see that Andrea had made a new friend. But when they gathered closer to where Andrea was sitting, the monkey saw them and bolted back into the forest. The group backed away a short distance, and the monkey returned, hopping back onto the table right next to Andrea, retrieving her hand and placing it on his back. It seemed to think that she was its "safe" person. The guests were amazed by Andrea—the ACTS tour guide and monkey whisperer!

Another wildlife encounter occurred when a professional mountain biking race was held in Kenya around Lake Nakuru. ACTS was hired to do the logistics. While the bikers raced, Andrea drove a truck loaded with tents and equipment to the next overnight campsite, sleeping in pup tents along the way.

Nature called one night while Andrea was in her tent, and she felt the need to respond. There was a portable latrine set up on the far edge of the camp, but she said to herself, *I'm not going to go all the way across the camp. I'm going to just go outside my tent into the woods and do a "bush pee."* So outside she went.

While out in the brush, she heard a loud noise that worried her. She had her phone with her, so she turned on the light and saw a huge hippopotamus staring right at her! She was in the middle of her "bush pee," so there wasn't much she could do. The hippo looked at her and went about his business, and she did the same.

Andrea's antics keep us laughing and praying. Although we were able to laugh off Andrea's encounters with animals, not all of her encounters were so innocent. Andrea learned this the hard way when she was studying in Dar es Salaam. She was living off campus at a professor's house with two other exchange students. They were told to always walk home together, but one particular day, Andrea's class ended late and her roommates were nowhere to be found. It was a pretty day and the streets looked crowded, so Andrea elected to make the five-block walk home alone.

Andrea started toward the house at a brisk pace, noticing that the number of people on the street seemed to thin out more the farther she walked. She felt uneasy as she crossed the street. She looked behind her and saw a teenage boy also crossing, although at a distance from her. Undeterred, Andrea pressed on toward her apartment.

A half block or so later, she sensed someone approaching, and she instinctively clutched her MacBook shoulder satchel tighter. Just then, the teen she had spotted earlier rushed forward and grabbed at her satchel, attempting to snatch it away from her while on the run. Andrea had a firm grip on the bag, so for a long moment or two, she and her assailant stared at each other eye to eye.

The two of them wrestled for the satchel, but Andrea refused to let go. That satchel meant everything to her. Not only was the laptop her means of completing her classroom assignments, but it was also her internet connection to her friends and family back home. She was not about to give it up without a fight, so she continued to tussle with the thug who was attempting to rob her.

Suddenly, the thief reached behind him and then started swinging a machete that he had pulled from his waistband. By adeptly maneuvering the satchel, Andrea was able to block his blows each time he swung the sharp blade. Eventually the thief was able to wrestle the satchel from Andrea, and he took off running down an alley.

Andrea continued on in tears but arrived at the professor's home with no further incident. Still, she was devastated. To her surprise, when she got to her room she saw her laptop computer sitting on her desk right where she had left it that morning. It was then that she realized that she had failed to put her laptop in the satchel before she went to class that morning.

Andrea later called home to tell us about the incident. We were shaken to hear about it but relieved that Andrea was fine. In recounting the incident, she said that she thought she might have been able to catch the crook if she had not been wearing flip-flops at the time he accosted her. *Well, thank God for those flip-flops!* I thought.

Upon reflection, I realized that this incident is a parable for so much of what we do in life. Sometimes we fight so hard to cling to what we think is important only to realize later that it wasn't. As I advised Andrea that day, sometimes the best thing to do in life is to just let go!

In more recent years, Andrea started her own aerial-silks business in Kenya. She had taken aerial silks as an exercise class at LSU (which is similar to that used by acrobats in shows such as Cirque du Soleil) and loved it. She started offering classes at gyms around Nairobi. Her business fits in with her mission of helping the people of Kenya because she is able to recruit impoverished street performers and hire them to work as instructors for her classes.

In September 2019, Darla and I visited Andrea in Kenya. "Why don't you open a studio in Brentwood and offer your classes there?" Darla asked, always dreaming of having her daughter back home.

"Why would I want to do that?" Andrea asked. "I live in Nairobi."

Message received, loud and clear.

People often ask Darla and me, "Is it dangerous? Aren't you worried about your daughter, a single young woman living on her own in Africa? How could you let her live there?" I reply that Andrea stopped listening to me when she was thirteen years old, even though I controlled the pocketbook then! There is no way I can control her now.

In all seriousness, we fully support Andrea. We want her to be happy, to do good, and to follow her calling, just as all parents want for their children. Even though we are thousands of miles apart, I feel closer to Andrea now more than ever. The connection that began to be restored during our first trip continues to grow as I see her living in her purpose and leading others to do the same.

After Andrea found peace within herself, she was able to reflect on her past. It turned out that she still felt some lingering hurt from the way some things were handled when she was going through her toughest times. In particular, there were occasions in high school when Andrea had displayed behavior and emotional outbursts that were not characteristic of her. In hindsight, these were cries for help, but Andrea remembers only odd looks and snide remarks from her teachers.

Andrea felt compelled to write to some of her former teachers to explain her actions at the time and to try to encourage them. She wanted them to understand why a good student might sometimes act out or lose interest in schoolwork. She wrote, "I'm not blaming anyone, but hopefully my experience will be helpful to you. I just wish that at least one teacher would have said something to me, just one teacher would have pulled me aside and asked, 'Andrea, is everything okay?' At least then I would have felt like someone cared."

These letters were therapeutic to Andrea, and thankfully, they were well-received by her teachers, leaving them encouraged and informed so that if any more Andreas come their way, they will have a better idea how to be there for them.

It has been so gratifying to see Andrea find her calling. I had prayed that our first trip to Rwanda would help rediscover the fun-loving, carefree girl who had been so impacted by the evil that found her on the Fourth of July so many years before. But I had underestimated the power of prayer and the redeeming nature of our Savior. In the months before that trip in 2009, my hopes and my spirits had sunk about as low as possible. Sometimes you have to hit rock bottom before you can get back up, but as our family journey shows, if God is your Rock, you can build from that foundation!

\\\

Similar to many Americans, Darla and I were ignorant of the horrendous sufferings endured by the Rwandan people in the 1994 genocide. To this day, I still cannot fully fathom what William, Ebralie, and their family went through and how they dealt with their suffering. Sadly, atrocities like those faced by the Mwizerwa family are repeated daily throughout our world. If we could all truly understand that God intends for us to be a family, that every person is made in His image, then perhaps we could find a way that such evil would never happen again. I surely hope so.

Our lives are still filled with peaks and valleys. Andrea's wounds and the destructive impact they reaped in our family led us to Rwanda, a land of peaks and valleys, where we discovered how precious life really is and how serving others brings healing to ourselves.

It is often hard to see God's love when we are suffering and facing *the valley of the shadow of death*, as the psalmist said (Psalm 23:4), but we have discovered that Jesus will never leave us, and He has promised that He will bring us *through* the valley.

All of our families were broken in some way. The Mwizerwa family was broken. Umuhoza's family was broken. Our own family was broken. However, we all trusted in a God who could put broken lives back together.

When you are going through a dark time in your life, you might feel that God has abandoned or forsaken you. I have discovered that if it seems He is not there, He has gone on ahead of us to lay a trail for us to follow. It is only when we look back that we can see that God's hand was indeed working in our situation, even when we were unaware of it. Although I had no clue what God was up to in our lives at the time, I can look back and easily see that He was moving in our family long before we realized.

When we filled out those Compassion sponsorship packets years ago and our six-year-old Andrea checked a box to sponsor a girl her age from Africa, it was totally random that we were assigned a young girl from Rwanda named Umuhoza. At that time, we could not yet have imagined that William and Ebralie and their family would become our neighbors in Brentwood, Tennessee. We certainly never would have thought that we would go on to visit Africa with such frequency, or that Andrea would end up building her life there.

God showed me over the course of three mission trips to Rwanda that He has something He wants to do in and through this story and through me. He allowed our family to be broken—beautifully broken—but He put the pieces back together in a beautiful pattern, similar to how a stained-glass window is made of broken segments of glass. In the hands of the Master, those jagged pieces are fashioned into something stronger, something new, something far more beautiful than they were before.

I have learned one thing for sure: helping others leads to healing. We can all touch people's lives if we permit God to use the experiences He has allowed us to go through to help heal somebody else. The amazing corollary is that in the process of being beautifully broken, we get healed as well.

I am just a financial planner—an ordinary guy who has never felt a calling to serve God as a pastor or a missionary—but God led me on a journey that revealed over and over again His presence in our lives and His desire to love and heal His children.

God knows why He had this ordinary guy put these stories in a book. I hope maybe I did it so that just the right person would read my story at just the right time, just as I read that letter from Umuhoza all those years ago. If our story can have the same sort of impact on that one person as that letter had on my family and me, then writing this book will have been worth it.

Epilogue

WHERE ARE THEY NOW?

William and Ebralie Mwizerwa live in Nashville, Tennessee, where they continue to work with Legacy Mission Village. Their son Tim, who was one year old at the time of the Rwandan genocide, graduated from Western Kentucky University and now works with his parents helping refugees and others at Legacy Mission Village. Tim's dynamic energy is a blessing to his parents and to the many refugees they help.

Andrea Hartley is in Nairobi, Kenya, guiding her own business, serving with ACTS, and living the life that God has designed for her to live. We know that what the Enemy meant for evil in her life, God has turned around and used for good.

Randy and Darla Hartley are still living in the same location in Brentwood. After Nate was born, Darla retired from her position as a pharmaceutical company representative. Randy continues working as a financial advisor and serves on the board of directors of Legacy Mission Village, working together with William and Ebralie to help other broken people.

The movie *Beautifully Broken* continues to be shown in numerous places around the world and is available for purchase. We receive letters or social media communications almost every week from people whose lives have been touched in meaningful ways because of the story. Only God knows why—but to Him belongs all glory!

Legacy Mission Village (LMV) is a 501(c)3 registered charity, which serves refugees from all over the world, helping them to assimilate successfully into American society. LMV offers a Kindergarten Readiness Program to prepare refugee children for school, a Journey Program to provide tutoring for high school refugee students, English as a Second Language classes for refugee parents, Citizenship classes to help our refugee community to become U.S. citizens, and countless other programs to help our refugee neighbors become successful members of our community. To find out more about Legacy Mission Village or to make a donation to help support the ministry, please visit www.LegacyMissionVillage.org.

ABOUT THE AUTHORS

Randy Hartley lives in Nashville, TN, where he has been a financial planner for thirty-eight years. Randy has been married to his wife, Darla, for thirty-five years. They have three children: Alyssa, Andrea, and Nate.

Randy served as executive producer for the film *Beautifully Broken*, which was released in 2018. Randy also produced the documentary *Through the Valley*, the true story upon which *Beautifully Broken* was based. *Through the Valley* won three film festival awards in 2014, including Documentary of the Year from the Religious Newswriters Association.

Randy serves as chairman of Legacy Mission Village, the refugee services charity founded by William and Ebralie Mwizerwa and whose origin is portrayed in the film and the book. Randy also serves on the board of a residential community for adults with developmental disabilities.

William and Ebralie Mwizerwa are founders of Legacy Mission Village, a refugee services ministry based in Nashville, TN. The ministry has helped thousands of refugees from all over the world to successfully integrate into American society. The Mwizerwas are themselves refugees from Rwanda. William and Ebralie have five children—Aimee, Myriam, Moses, Tim and David.

Ken Abraham is a *New York Times* best-selling author, known around the world for his collaborations with popular celebrities and fascinating, high-profile public figures such as astronaut Buzz Aldrin, megachurch minister Joel Osteen; actor Chuck Norris; 9/11 widow Lisa Beamer; NFL football coach and NASCAR team owner Joe Gibbs; former U.S. Attorney General John Ashcroft, Senator Bob Dole; Neil Clark Warren, psychologist and founder of e-Harmony.com; former U.S. Senate Majority Leader and heart transplant surgeon Bill Frist; champion boxer and entrepreneur George Foreman; former U.S. Attorney General Alberto R. Gonzales; country music icon Randy Travis; and ASCAP's gospel songwriter of the century Bill Gaither.

Fifteen books on which Ken has collaborated have appeared on the *New York Times* bestsellers lists, with three of Ken's works reaching the number one position.

Ken wrote the *New York Times* bestseller *Walk to Beautiful* with country music artist Jimmy Wayne, a former foster child who walked 1,700 miles across America to raise awareness about foster kids.

Ken's most recent *New York Times* bestsellers include *No Dream Is Too High*, with Apollo 11 astronaut Buzz Aldrin; and *More Than Rivals*, a gripping story of racial conflict and reconciliation, based on actual events.

At present, Ken has more than twelve million books in print.

ENDNOTES

CHAPTER 10

1 Steve Bradshaw and Ben Loeterman, "The Triumph of Evil," January 26, 1999, PBS Frontline, https://www.pbs.org/wgbh/pages/frontline/shows/evil/.

CHAPTER 11

2 Steve Bradshaw, "The Triumph of Evil."